Leaders Don't Command

Inspire Growth, Ingenuity,
and Collaboration

Jorge Cuervo
Translated from the Spanish edition by
Sergio Domínguez/Fast Lines, Inc.

PRESS

Originally published as *Mejor liderar que mandar*
© Libros de Cabecera and Jorge Cuervo, 2012

28 27 26 25 24   3 4 5

ATD Press is an internationally renowned source of insightful and practical information on talent development, workplace learning, and professional development.

ATD Press
1640 King Street
Alexandria, VA 22314 USA

Ordering information: Books published by ATD Press can be purchased by visiting ATD's website at www.td.org/books or by calling 800.628.2783 or 703.683.8100.

Library of Congress Control Number: 2015932219

ISBN-10: 1-56286-935-3
ISBN-13: 978-1-56286-935-9
e-ISBN: 978-1-60728-497-0

ATD Press Editorial Staff
Director: Kristine Luecker
Manager: Christian Green
Community of Practice Manager, Human Capital: Ann Parker
Associate Editors: Melissa Jones and Sarah Cough
Cover Design: Lon Levy
Text Design: Maggie Hyde
Printed by BR Printers, San Jose, CA

Contents

Foreword

In times of crisis like those we have seen recently, leadership—or the lack thereof—often serves as an easy target to offload people's frustrations about who is responsible for the situation. Among the usual suspects are politicians, business owners, and managers. Discussions on the topic show that leadership is a multifaceted and complex social phenomenon that supports multiple approaches. In these circumstances it is always a good idea for someone to make the effort to bring some common sense to the discussion. It is important to break down and update existing opinions on the topic and provide some practical suggestions for those who want to improve their own leadership skills.

This book by Jorge Cuervo does just that, cleverly exploiting a combination of the author's own experiences as an executive, trainer, and coach, and showing an undeniable talent for translating that experience into an easy and enjoyable read.

Reading the book has made me reflect on what we teach about leadership and how we can learn from and improve upon it. I will focus on two issues that I consider to be particularly significant: the role of influence and the importance of introspection in the development of leadership skills.

Gary Yukl, one of the foremost leadership scholars, has counted more than 1,500 different definitions of the term *leadership*. Despite this enormous diversity of meanings, many of them have some common characteristics: Leadership is a type of relationship that has to do with influencing others in the service of a project or common objective. Influence, then, is a key element in leadership, but it is too often viewed as something external. It is often seen as a quality of the relationship between the one exercising leadership and those to whom it is addressed. To understand the effectiveness of this type of relationship it is more important to focus on the internal effects that it has on different people.

A great ESADE Business School professor and an old friend, Paco Vila-hur has pointed out in his lectures that "to influence" means to cause fluidity or flow—to stir something inside people to get to an answer that appeals to the rational and emotional dimensions of the human mind. Now, you can obviously either bring out the best in people or awaken the worst of their demons. Seeing this distinction allows us to recognize the difference between good and bad leadership.

We should be wary of managers who deny their desire to influence others because that is the essence of leadership. They tend to be people who believe in the ability to dissociate the rational from the emotional. They believe in checking their baggage at the door. Based on discoveries in the field of neuro-science in the past two decades, Cuervo reminds us that this is biologically impossible. Managers may also be people who ascribe a negative connotation to influence, likening it to manipulation. This attitude is partially responsible for people's negative perception of the word *leadership*, which is fueled by too many disgraceful examples where the ability to influence has been used to serve spurious and transparent interests.

Indeed, the line between influence and manipulation—which can be very thin—becomes clear when we ask ourselves about the intentions and underlying values. Here we find the freedom to accept or reject an idea, or to adhere to the project or not.

Despite all the criticism, companies and individual managers continue to invest millions of dollars a year in leadership development. Receiving an adequate return on this investment is a major challenge, and means walking a path fraught with obstacles that are rooted in widespread ideas and beliefs. Cuervo refutes some of these beliefs and proposes many tools to pave the way.

One such idea is to look within yourself. In a celebrated article, Kay Peters highlighted the four stages that lead to maturity in management development: learning management techniques, understanding the strategy, exercising leadership, and self-discovery, including a sense that one's own actions are in the service of others. The message here, with an air of classicism, becomes "the improvement of leadership based on the improvement of self-leadership."

This call for introspection, also reflected in Richard Boyatzis's intentional change model, which Cuervo recognizes as a source of inspiration, is a call for executives to invest some of their invaluable time for thinking about themselves—to catch their breath, reorient, and reprioritize. Paradoxically, this self-reflective retreat creates the conditions for the reconstruction of a more open and selfless leadership model. As Cuervo points out, taking inspiration from Rafael Echeverria, one way to understand leadership is to think of it as a group quality and survival tool, from a sense of freedom of action that provides full awareness of the temporary situation and the privilege that playing the role of leader signifies.

In these times of crisis, Joseph Badaracco's advice takes on renewed importance. He proposed that we benefit more from the combined work of many hardworking and discreet leaders than a few heroic and singular acts of leadership. Cuervo's book is a good tool for those leaders who seek continuous improvement in the performance of their complex responsibilities.

Ricard Serlavós
Associate Professor, People Management and Organization
ESADE Universitat Ramon Llull

Preface

I started to write this book with what seemed like a clear objective: to connect current leadership theory with my own professional experience in a way that provided a map to help aspiring leaders face personal and professional challenges.

In short, I set out to write something that readers would find useful.

This process is the result of my own personal evolution, one that quickly uncovered a problem: Too many years of writing reports, memos, and briefings leave a mark. Accept it, Jorge. You are a boring writer.

I was afraid people wouldn't even make it past page four. Four? Really? Nope! Not even page two!

I felt the cortisol gushing through my veins with the fear of a blank page. The ideas that flowed freely in speech now rattled around in my head chaotically, full of dynamically complex interconnections and consequences. I couldn't make sense of it all in a way that someone else could understand. I would fail.

Even my plump little ego, which thus far had given me the strength to go through this challenge, now grew thin and started to work against me: "Give it up. Don't risk the embarrassment." I called a meeting of all of my "inner Jorges" and asked them for help. This is my team:

- **Jorge number one** is the tech. He is rational, methodical, and academic. He needs order and proof for everything. Solid and boring, he doesn't worry much about good impressions. He has a degree in pharmaceutical sciences and an MBA. Life quickly put him on the back burner. In my head, he wears a white lab coat.

- **Jorge number two** arose when the former proved himself boring. He picked up the baton and took control. He's the aggressive executive: ambitious, dominant, and resourceful. He enjoys achievement and the thrill of a challenge. He wants results and won't tolerate nonsense. His dream is to be the general manager of something big. He has an enormous and wild ego. He loves expensive suits and is not averse to a good tie (clearly, there are preppy tendencies). Some value him while others can't stand his arrogance, but we should be understanding. Deep down he has an enormous need for acceptance and acknowledgment. A lot of his strength comes from those vulnerabilities, and he sees his job as a way of overcoming them. He's not a bad guy, just a little overwhelming. I try to space out his appearances because empathy isn't his strong suit.

- **Jorge number three** is the consultant. He's a lot like Jorge number two only more sensible and a better listener. He's also a bit like Jorge number one in his analytical and scientific spirit. He lives in the same world as Jorge number two, but moves through it more slowly. He's more of an observer than a man of action. He sees things from the outside and is less ambitious. He wears a suit and tie, but adds an informal touch to his ensemble. He struggles to stay in control under pressure from Jorge number two, who shows up like a whirlwind. Jorge number three has found that at its core, his job is to answer three questions:

  - Why don't people do what they're told?
  - Why don't people do what they say they'll do?
  - Why don't people do what's best for them?

Answering them is only half the solution. The other half is another story. In any case, he's found that he is interested in people, and wants to help them but doesn't know how. What he has learned about organizational management makes a lot of sense, but in practice things always get complicated and turn out differently than he expected. Jorge number three seems constantly puzzled and gets the feeling that there's something beneath the organization that escapes him.

- **Jorge number four** is the professor. He was born a bit out of necessity and is connected with something deeply rooted in my nature. He likes to see how people can grow and is driven by the occasional sense of gratitude he gets from them. Training people gives my life meaning and Jorge number four is the incarnation of that. However, I didn't know any of this when he showed up. It was a complete surprise.

  Jorge number four is simpler than the previous iterations. He wants to connect with his students from his being, not his ego. He really likes what he does even though it's often exhausting. Jorge number four dresses casually and adapts well to his surroundings, depending on the battlefield. He likes feisty audiences and enjoys surprising people. He's a bit of a provocateur. What really gets him going deep down, more than dispensing knowledge, is awakening a desire to learn in his students. He's fine with being a doorman (opening doors for people): Some will walk through them and others won't.

  Jorge number four is always amazed at how little humans learn, how much effort it takes us, and how much we can do with the little bits we get! Since coming to this realization, Jorge number four tells his students to be on their toes so that those few things that they learn are truly relevant to their lives.

- **Jorge number five**, the coach, was the last one to show up. He is the result of the collaboration between Jorge number three and Jorge number four to find ways to help bring about change in people. He's happy coaching, but he isn't a fundamentalist—if one day he finds a method that's more effective, he will gladly incorporate it into his repertoire and unlearn whatever he needs to. Jorge number five is the perpetual student, the one who truly loves to learn. Still, he is not free from occasionally having to fight off his ego.

Lately, he works more and more with Jorge number four in his courses. They get along well, are happy with their results, and make a good team. They aren't sure how far this collaboration will go but are willing to give it a shot.

This is the team I recruited to write these pages. They are fighters who aren't afraid to roll up their sleeves! They don't always agree, but people say that a spirited debate is healthy, right? I guess we'll see. In any event, you hold the result in your hands and it is you who will determine its success.

But what's that? Someone else approaches? Will there be a Jorge number six?

Introduction

> Executive leadership quality can explain as much as
> 45 percent of an organization's performance.
> —Day and Lord (1988)

"Companies do not get the most out of their people" (Michaels, Handfield-Jones, and Axelrod 2001). When executives were asked if their companies developed their people well, only 3 percent responded positively!

Something is up. If you're a manager or business owner, you know full well that your job has become an extremely high-risk activity, as much a risk to your professional career as your health. This was not always the case. But today the first decision a manager has to face is "can I apply my previous experience here? And, if so, to what extent?" Managers are fighting the greatest dose of uncertainty in history and so are their teams.

From Hominid to Man

The root of this problem stretches back to millions of years ago when an adventurous primate descended from a tree in the African bush and began the journey of man. Our ancestors may seem, at first glance, to have been rather defenseless in that environment without powerful jaws or sharp claws.

Their chances for survival seemed grim. But they overcame their obstacles and we are the product of their success! Although I sometimes look around me and am overcome by doubt.

They survived because they developed three key skills: the ingenuity to find creative solutions, the power to act as a group, and, above all, the will to survive at all costs. And each of those skills resided in their brain. We are who we are today because of a survival-oriented brain. That is its function, its raison d'être, not the pursuit of truth or achievement of happiness. Yes, we can use it for that, too, but our brain was not sculpted by evolution for those ends. If we want to use it for that purpose we will have to learn to reprogram it, because we did not come factory-equipped with the necessary software. We have to develop it.

In short, our brain is a tool that is both powerful and fragile, one that we barely know how to adequately manage to meet the challenges of our times. In the past it has allowed us to extend our lifespan, as well as create a world so full of uncertainty and change that it is testing the limits of our own ability to adapt to it.

The same brain that once commanded a hoard of tribal warriors is now in charge of a nuclear fleet—or a bank!

That explains a lot, right? Spectacular advances in neuroscience highlight the limitations of our very nature to successfully confront the world we've created, at times with more ambition than conscience. Authors such as Antonio Damasio, recipient of the Prince of Asturias Award for Technical and Scientific Research in 2005, have torn down some of the basic paradigms that much of our thinking is built on. For example, the classical definition of the human being has changed from that of a rational being to a "being that rationalizes over an emotional base."

Reason and Emotion

Today we know that it is not possible to make decisions and carry them out without emotion. In fact, it is the root of our success as a species. Understand success in the strictest biological sense as the ability to proliferate. For the most part, the discoveries that have changed our perception of human potential were produced during the first decade of the 21st century, although they have yet to make it into the management of organizations in any significant way. We continue going about projects as we always have: an authority develops an allegedly rational plan that came from a small number of brains, which is then implanted into the organization.

Don't we realize that the concept of implantation implies violence? It is surgical, metallic, and applied by force. The missing piece of this puzzle—which some may even call the victim—is the individual, the one responsible for making our plan work! Isn't that where the floodwaters that capsize our projects come from? The current organizational environment is the most complex it has ever been; we must apply new understanding to it so that we can turn the way we manage organizations around.

Some things have no name in accounting. And we all know that which has no name does not exist. We have a place in our ledgers for personnel costs but not lack of motivation, lack of incentive, debilitating routines, or lost opportunities. These costs do exist. They are real but they are camouflaged elsewhere and because of that are never incorporated into the organization's executive consciousness. You manage what you know. What you don't know manages you!

In a time of accelerated change—one that is simultaneously fascinating and stressful—in which paradigms are constantly being revised, traditional safety nets guarantee nothing. Today, organizational survival depends on successfully managing three factors:

- innovation and creativity
- flexibility in the face of change
- client relationships.

Whether you are innovating, actively adapting, or properly caring for your clients, every member of the organization, including those who do not participate directly in these areas, must go beyond simply doing their jobs. They must want to do them. And if they enjoy doing them, all the better. That "wanting to do things" is what we call attitude. Without it there is no commitment. Without commitment there are no positive results. That "wanting to do things" attitude is the key to the survival of the company: Whether we are ready to see it or not, the difference between the life and death of the organization is marked increasingly by the human factor, and not by viewing humans as resources. That is why the times we live in are so harsh to our management style!

Today's managers are not worse than those of the past, but it sure feels like we are. We face a completely new environment—one that is much more demanding—and we are armed with concepts and tools from the 20th century, maybe even the 19th century. Complexity makes uncertainty permeate all situations in life, and traditional parameters that up until now have defined a good manager are proving insufficient.

> An environment filled with this much uncertainty demands a leadership style that will inspire, encourage, and develop attitudes in teams that equip them to confront it. We will see that this is exactly the same as saying more and better leadership.

Acting like a leader today is much more necessary and difficult, requiring more commitment than in any other time in recorded history. It is not enough to get our teams to put their hands to work. We also need them to include their hearts and minds. And the difficulties that our teams experience in this environment have to be overcome first.

Managers Are Not Always Leaders

Without a doubt, these days being a manager does not automatically mean being a leader. That should be the case, of course. Leadership should permeate the entire management function, but this requires personal dedication and specific and constant training by the people in that role. These complex times that we live in, which are a result of rapid change, demand better people management skills, starting with those who manage others.

Those of us who have years of team management and consulting experience can attest that people tend to use only a fraction of their potential at work. For instance, I remember a series of change management workshops that we ran in a multinational company with a good reputation in the technology sector. The exercise required several different groups to design a change management project that met a set of predefined parameters. The groups that consisted of unspecialized workers came up with proposals of the same high quality as those in groups that included managers, even though the unspecialized workers used less technical language. The hardest part for us was convincing them that they were capable of doing it. They at first refused to even try, frustrated by years of discouragement, and were surprised by the results. Some were even upset and claimed that they would have preferred not to have found out! By the end of the workshop, we concluded that they needed quality leadership that would make them believe in their own abilities.

Managing talent is the key competitive factor. We go to great lengths to find and keep it. And yet there are untapped wells of squandered talent in the very same companies that are desperately looking for it outside. Do we think talent does not exist because we do not know how to extract it?

In order to do that, we have to know and develop our understanding of how we operate—starting with ourselves. We can then mobilize those three levers that have been the key to the survival of our species: the capacity for ingenuity, teamwork, and the will to survive. These keys are also the basis for success in business.

Studies are constantly being published that tie leadership to organizational results and the market even offers methodological tools to evaluate the quality of that leadership. It has been proven that leadership development makes the difference by accomplishing several goals, including mobilizing existing knowledge in different levels of the organization, involving people and increasing their commitment, fostering follow-through and communication, and managing resistance to change by transforming it into initiative and creativity. OK, that sounds great! But how do you do it?

There are a lot of ways to do it, and they all follow the same paradigm shift: Move from "get people to do" to "get people to want to do." And, as we have seen, the art of "getting people to want" has a name: leadership. The book that you have in your hands was written with the aim of helping you create and follow your own path as a leader.

Our challenge as managers is to awaken and mobilize our capacity for leadership so that we can cultivate that true well of competitive advantage. For many companies, this will mean modifying corporate culture and, above all, overcoming our traditional tendency toward more authoritative management styles. We will have to learn and unlearn. We will become more competitive and—in all probability—also better people.

Yes, it is a difficult road that we set out on because it also takes us deeper within ourselves. But the stakes are worth the effort and the rewards are gigantic. Not only will we bring our teams to succeed in the complex environments that we find ourselves in today, ones fraught with uncertainty, but we will also go through the rewarding process of professional and personal growth.

How to Use This Book

As I explained earlier, the objective of this work is to help readers construct their own map to navigate the foggy world of leadership and, thus, get maximum practical use. To that end, my first recommendation is to start by following the central pillars—start from the beginning. This book is broken down into three distinct parts. Part I shows the essence of leadership and the emotional processes that influence it. Thus it is essential to the meaning of the following two parts.

However, from that moment on, even though the book has a logical structure, you can follow any order you please. The relationship between leadership and logical reason is indirect. And sometimes we need to delve deeper into a certain topic that at that moment seems pressing to us. For this reason, the chapters in Parts II and III are written in a way that, while fitting in a natural order, will also hold up as independent sections.

Part II, Ideas That Do Not Help, looks to dismantle a series of beliefs and stereotypes that hold a lot of weight in our world, but often lack real meaning and hinder the development of leadership. Part III contains what I call leadership tools, and answers the question, "What can I do to improve my own leadership skills?"

In the beginning of this section I used the word *map* deliberately: Experience has taught me that leadership is not a place suited for cookbooks. The same recipe applied to different people and different circumstances will no doubt yield different results. So my second recommendation—and the most important one—is that rather than learning new skills, you must make them your own. Experiment and find yourself in the process. I suggest that you read this book with an explorer's spirit, one that goes into unknown territory to discover its secrets and who, not just focusing on the goal, also enjoys the adventure. So grab your safari hat and go!

PART I

Understanding Leadership

What the Heck Is Leadership?

"With all this talk of leadership, the articles and studies, it seems to be in fashion and, frankly, I am a little tired of it."

Many professionals are starting to feel this way and it's not surprising. Leadership supports many different approaches and is an evocative field that often attracts controversy. Essentially, the same thing happens in advertising. You get the feeling that everyone is expressing themselves emphatically, but would we be able to define leadership plainly and practically?

Humans are storytelling monkeys. For countless generations we have gathered around the campfire telling tales and myths designed to solidify our group cohesion, tribal values, and personal abilities. In those stories the hero figure is always the key element, serving as the example and point of reference. This perspective has always pervaded the study of leadership. Throughout history, science and philosophy have dedicated a lot of attention to it, but almost always from the point of view of the supposed protagonist, the leader himself: What is he like? What does he do in the various situations he is up against? What attitudes do we see in him? How does he communicate?

Scholars have given a lot of thought to the characteristics of the leader. And this has ultimately proven itself to be a dead end. Over time, there have been as many leadership styles as there have been leaders studied. We have seen leaders who are extroverts and introverts, emotional and cold, charismatic and dull, men and women, gay and straight, tall and short, of average stature, and the list goes on. And what was the conclusion? The study of a leader's mere characteristics does not lead us to any valid general model.

However, in the last two decades advances in social psychology and neuroscience have provided new insights that are much more enlightening because they reveal how human relationships actually work. The keys in this process have come from developing the concept of emotional intelligence based on the contributions of Daniel Goleman and the application of systems theory to human groups. From this we now know that leadership is naturally relational and is a role of the system.

I especially like the approach by Goleman, Boyatzis, and McKee in their book *Primal Leadership* (2002), where they state that leadership is a relationship! Leadership is one type of human relationship in which some people put their trust in another who they feel is the most qualified—who we call the leader—to guide the group toward achieving a common goal. Let's not forget that the word *leader* also means guide.

A leader is responsible for a variety of very worthwhile tasks. For example, keeping the group energized; giving the task at hand meaning and bringing it to life; developing his or her own abilities, including driving people to go beyond what they thought was possible; learning to learn, a process that implies knowing how to fail exceptionally well; and, especially, managing egos so that the value of the collective prevails over that of the individual. And that's just the beginning. There is so much more to it, but we will get to that.

Great! Count me in! What do you have to do to be a leader? Where do you learn all of that? What techniques do you have to master?

Well, we are at the beginning of that journey and this is where the difficulties start to become clear. The training ground will be one of managing emotions in a relational framework. We know that managing human relationships is a complicated work. Let's be frank. If you have management experience, how many times have you thought to yourself, "why did I get myself into this? I wish they were robots!" Be honest with yourself when you answer. Self-awareness is one of the most important foundations of leadership.

I get people who come to my professional development courses looking for techniques to help them manage people. Essentially, they want to know how to change others and influence their behavior without having to change themselves. Bad news! Leadership is not for you, but don't fret; there are other paths out there.

> "Duty is what one expects from others."
> —Oscar Wilde, *A Woman of No Importance*

Imagine that you go to a store, and with your change the clerk gives you a coin that has a different-sized face on each side and neither side matches up. Would you accept it? Of course not! You would think it was defective or some sort of crazy counterfeit and you would demand a different coin. Leadership is similar: One side of the coin is self-leadership, which is the capacity to manage yourself; the other side is leading others, which is the capacity to influence others and get them to follow you voluntarily.

Are you giving people a coin with oddly sized faces? Is your self-leadership as highly developed as the skills you expect of others? It would seem that being a leader is the "it" thing to try these days; that is, until they come to this rude awakening.

Listen up. There are personal and professional growth opportunities here! Leadership requires effort and the reward is personal development and learning. If you, using your influence as a leader, want others to do things differently, you'll have to start doing things differently yourself. You will have to be the first to change and you will have to like it! Are you starting to see why being a leader is so challenging and why there are so few good ones?

Oh! By the way, just doing your homework does not guarantee that your team will buy your idea. It is completely possible that despite how right you may be, the group will not follow and you will not achieve leadership. Every good leader knows it. To be a true leader you have to be willing to risk your leadership. Mediocre leaders refuse to accept this reality and end up betraying their very essence as leaders and as people.

This situation is depicted very well in Clint Eastwood's *Invictus*. The film tells the story, based on real events, of how Nelson Mandela was able to change a 1995 world rugby championship celebrated in South Africa into a tipping point for the whole country to unite around a symbol—its own national team.

At that time, South Africa was going through the fragile start of a new democratic system upon which sat, for the first time, the basis of a peaceful and equal coexistence among all its citizens, whatever their ethnicity and language. The hope was that they could overcome the long and painful period of apartheid rule. Powerful forces wanted the project to fail, fueled by the ballast of cultural differences, the fear of the future, and the scars of years of conflict. In short, the whole country was a tinderbox that many arsonists called their home.

Despite having suffered cruel treatment during more than 27 years in jail, Mandela was able to see the importance of overcoming hatred and fear in order to achieve something miraculous: to get past the tense coexistence and get everyone to commit to a common future. And so he had the wild idea of using the Rugby World Cup, which his country was hosting, to symbolize and ritualize the new South Africa he dreamed of—in his own words, "a rainbow nation"—a place where everyone of every color could live in harmony.

The objective seemed insane. Rugby was still "the white man's sport" and the national team, the Springboks, named after a species of African gazelle, had come to be known as a real symbol of apartheid's bloody oppression. The more hostile elements of the black opposition had even tried, with some degree of success, to boycott the team's international travel. And Mandela sought nothing less than to unite everyone around such a monster. Even within the African National Congress (ANC), his own party, people were considering dissolving the team and erasing all traces of it from existence.

In a key scene in the film, Mandela attends a meeting about the team's dissolution and manages to convince the assembly against it, essentially opening the door for his plans. But on his way to the meeting his assistant asked, "You know this idea could cost you your job, right?" He simply replied, "The day that stops me is the day I am no longer fit to lead." It is that conviction that gives him the power to defend his point of view so vigorously and justly. How would he have acted if he were afraid of losing his job? How rare is that type of action in business and politics!

> That which you fear losing does not belong to you—you belong to it.

Good leadership requires an abundance of two values:

- One quality is the humility to understand and accept that leadership is not a quality you own, but rather a pact made between the group and the leader. When the group stops buying what the leader is selling, it replaces it with another. In reality, leadership is the team's job! It is not something you have, but rather something you do.

- The other value is the generosity to accept the former and still work for the good of the group above your own interest and ego.

Yes, in leadership, too, there are qualifiers: The presence of these two values is the defining quality of good leadership. However, if you were not interested in making this effort, don't worry. Being a leader is not mandatory! There is another road that may interest you: you could focus on being a good boss, which we will explain later.

A Practical Definition of a Leader

Drawing on our experience, let's establish a practical definition of what a leader is. To that end, our baseline concept will be: *A leader is the person that receives from others the trust to guide them in the pursuit of what they feel is the best possible solution from a specific initial context.* Now let's dissect that definition:

"A leader is the person . . . " As we have cited already, leadership is a type of human relationship and, as such, runs between the emotional connections from one individual to another. As a result, only people can lead, not organizations. This is because organizations lack a limbic system. Sometimes in the press you read about, for example, "the movement led by Greenpeace" or "the campaign led by the UN for. . ." They are acceptable as metaphors, but don't let that confuse you. Leadership is a phenomenon that occurs among people.

". . . that receives from others the trust . . . " In the ever practical Western culture, a leader is simply someone who has followers. There is a lot of truth behind that idea because it is the people who follow that make the leader. Leadership is not something that someone has, but rather something that others give to that person and can also take away. Also, trust is given to the person who they feel deserves it, which is not always the person who tells you what you want to hear, but rather the person who proves himself to be genuine. We will look into this further later.

". . . to guide them in the pursuit . . . " As we have already stated, the word leader means guide. A guide shows you the way, knows how to orient herself, encourages, and so on. She will not walk for you. Solving your problems is not expected of true, quality leadership. Instead, true leadership puts you on the path toward something you want to achieve and sometimes even helps you discover what you want to achieve! Those who are leaders will always take an active role in success, but they will have to do the walking themselves. And they will often want the leader to take them beyond what they believe to be their limits. Leadership can bring you toward inspiration, as well as personal and professional growth, which will be greater the more effort you put into it.

At this point we have to put up our caution signs for politicians and average citizens alike: Only mediocre leadership carried out by mediocre leaders who guide mediocre people believe that their function is to provide well-being. This is very important. Quality leadership brings out the best in us, drives us forward, and makes us put in the effort and take an active role in things.

In contrast, poor leadership sells us comfort and well-being. And when we as citizens buy into it we become as mediocre as those who sell it. When we set out to hike to the summit, we must do so knowing that fatigue and effort are coming with us, and that is the fundamental meaning of what we are going to learn here. Comfort seekers need not apply.

"**. . . of what they feel . . .**" Do not be fooled. We have already reiterated that emotion is the vehicle for leadership. As such, in order to lead, you should equip yourself with facts and rational arguments as long as you get people to feel them. It is not about convincing, but rather mobilizing, and that can only be done on an emotional level. Remember the famous speech by Martin Luther King Jr., champion of the fight against discrimination in the United States, a man who gave his life for what he believed: "I have a dream." Can you imagine that speech if it had started with "this year I promise to reduce racial discrimination by 8.2 percent?"

If you expect other people to feel what you are proposing, you must feel it first. If you believe in what you're saying, you can communicate it effectively. The rest is just technique, which is teachable. But if you do not feel it, no measure of technique will make a difference, and your message will not make it into people's hearts. Humans are good at detecting inconsistencies and being skeptical. We have been doing it for millennia.

Good leadership must use its head even if it is born in the heart. If you, as was the case for me, have a background in scientific or technical study, be aware that you have been taught to undervalue the emotional and you may have to unlearn some of that in order to improve your people management skills. It is difficult to do without help, and any investment that leads to a good coaching program is one you cannot put a price on. As the Canadian philosopher Marshall McLuhan said, the message is the medium and you are the medium, and support, of your own message. Believe in what you do and be genuine. The rest is a matter of technique.

". . . is the best possible solution . . ." As John Kotter, professor emeritus at Harvard Business School, pointed out, to get one human group going it is necessary to develop awareness of a need. That is to say, the group must be aware that it is confronting an inexorable change and that it should accept it as such. Inexorable is the key word. You could arrive at this as the result of some pressing problem, from a strong desire to improve your situation, or any combination of the two. The ability of the leader to develop an awareness of need in the group and to drive it toward acceptance are key elements of leadership.

". . . from a specific initial context." If leadership is a relationship, by its very nature it will experience situations or contexts that condition it. Ultimately, leadership is subject to the laws of any human relationship. For example, you undoubtedly have friends that are great for going to the theater, but you might not go to a nightclub or a sporting event with them. The same thing happens in the world of leadership. Much of it depends on context. The following is a very intuitive, and real, example that I use in my classes.

Imagine a group of friends that are playing in a soccer tournament. Out on the field, one of them moves the ball along very well, can read plays, and can motivate the rest of the team. He is a genuine leader. The game ends and this victorious team decides to celebrate, only to realize that their athletic leader is pretty dull and antisocial after hours. Now, there is another member of the team who is no star on the field but he is a connector, to borrow a term from Malcolm Gladwell. He knows the bouncers at all the best nightclubs in town and can really break the ice with the ladies. Do we start to see who will be the leader in this new setting?

> The important thing is that the team has leadership, and not necessarily that you are the leader of the team.

Leadership is a function of the group. It is not the property of one specific person. In systemic terms, leadership is simply a role of the system! For a period of time you may assume the role of acting leader, but changes in context can cause the system to replace you with someone else. So pushing ego aside, we understand that leadership is not our own characteristic or something that we own. It is something that the human system lets us borrow, and if conditions change, it will go to someone who is deemed a better fit. A leader's decline starts when he is driven by ego and believes that leadership is his exclusive property, because to do so interrupts the flow of leadership within the system.

Context divides leadership into zones:

- **Functional:** Like in the soccer team example, depending on the activity the group is involved in, one leader may be preferable to another.

- **Cultural:** It may be possible for you to get along with people in your hometown or your current city, and be unable to connect with or lead people in some city halfway around the world. Or maybe it is easier for you to lead a group of salespeople than production technicians because they belong to different business subcultures.

- **Personal:** You've developed a strong capacity for leadership. Still, there are times in your life, perhaps times of personal crisis, when you find it difficult to inspire trust in others. Or perhaps you know someone who was a strong leader as a child, but not so much as an adult.

Leadership Comes From the Whole Person

The definition of a leader that we've established and dissected is built from a practical perspective, maybe even a mechanical one. However, there are other possible approaches and now we will visit one that is particularly transcendent. We'll start from the essential function of leadership, the thing that gives it meaning, which is the ability to get the group to give its best in certain situations. To do so, you should:

- Develop awareness of a need.

- Get the group to accept the situation.

- Encourage the development of a proactive attitude.

- Make energy and awareness flow from one individual to another.

- Achieve collaborative synergy between the group.

- Encourage continuous feedback between members of the group so that they can turn failures into learning opportunities and successes into celebrations.

- Manage conflicts in a constructive way.

I like to express this in a less rational and more concise way: Leadership is the art of getting people to want to do things. I find the word *art* to be very attractive because it requires combining technique with that intangible, almost magical, element known as talent. Talent is the human matter over which technique is suspended: The same technique applied by different people or at different times will yield different results!

Let's take a look at a concrete example: If I buy a book of recipes by Ferran Adrià, considered by many to be the world's greatest chef, will I become Ferran Adrià? Of course not. To become a chef I would have to gain knowledge, try different techniques, study ingredients, know which ones to substitute for others, and so on. I would have to create. I would have to learn to master the arena, which is to say, gain mastery over it.

That process would not only require me to work on cooking, but also to work on myself. In parallel, I would have personally evolved, learned to discipline myself, subjected myself to criticism, taken risks, learned to fail well and to persevere, learned my limits and challenged them, and questioned and reinvented myself. I would become a master. So mastery requires the combination of both processes—knowledge and technique—to be executed effectively. It's a state of being. For an example take this extract from *Weapon of Life: Zen and the Traditional Art of the Samurai* (1983):

> To be a master does not mean to believe that one has reached the hierarchical peak of knowledge but rather that, in the true meaning of the term, it is a way of life that implies a certain state of being. He who undertakes the way of the master discovers that nothing truly belongs to him. This quest usually causes him, on a day-to-day level, to peel off layers. . . . The master's singular vocation is to impart knowledge. Therefore, he must dispense the generosity that comes with it. . . . Service is the key word that conditions his existence. If his character traits do not correspond in some way with this picture, unlikely is it that he who teaches will have understood the humanism that his teaching holds. . . . Knowledge is not absorbed in a few gestures nor in a few scattered words. It is a commitment of the entire being.

When applying this comparison to the world of leadership the same thing happens: good leadership is practiced by the person that I currently am, having been prepared as a human being to practice it, and to let it go when playing that role is no longer my responsibility, without selfishness and without self-centeredness, taking only the good of the group into consideration. This gives leadership a closer relationship with personal growth than with techniques or skills. They are useless without adequate personal preparation! To undertake leadership with conscience you must be prepared. At the same time, however, leadership itself is an authentic school of human development. That's why it has become a coveted role that justifies such widespread editorial and scholastic coverage that it's starting to bore us all to death. Like so many things of which much is spoken, little is actually done!

Humanity has been aware of this connection between what we do and what we are since the dawn of time. It used to be just as important for being an artisan master as it was for being a farmer. This was the way things worked for thousands of years. It is only now that we distinguish knowledge from personal evolution in many aspects of our lives.

So Then, Is a Leader Born or Made?

When I ask this question in my classes, the responses are always rather divided, with a slight majority in those who think a leader is made. It makes sense because we're dealing with people taking leadership classes! Those who believe that a leader is made believe that leadership can be learned, so taking a series of courses to achieve it makes sense. But the truly interesting thing is that we also get a lot of people who believe that leaders are born that way. If leaders are born that way and you already are one, then you should have that characteristic your entire life.

But if you aren't a leader, what can you do? And what makes a person who believes such a thing sign up for a course on leadership in the first place?

Maybe leadership is such an evocative topic that it generates curiosity in and of itself. A lot of people want to understand what is happening in the world today and figure that exploring leadership can shed some light on things. It would be a very fortunate assumption given that developing leadership means deepening your knowledge of people and, especially, of yourself.

Historically speaking, science has also failed to provide an answer to this question. With the genetics boom of the latter half of the 20th century, everything was suddenly explainable through genetics. Then in the 1990s when emotional intelligence research started to gain traction, everything seemed to be related to education and learning. And now, the dominant trend puts it, more or less, halfway between the two.

There is a wide body of opinion, which I subscribe to, that binds those who think both answers are correct. A leader is probably born with certain skills that, in early life, allow the person to develop a solid base of self-management and interpersonal communication and that, later in life, are enriched with learning and experience. Or not. Something similar happens with other more tangible skills. Some people are born physically stronger or faster than others, but those who aren't can go to a gym and work on those features. Some great athletes started in their discipline to overcome a physical deficiency or illness, but there are also those to whom certain things just came easily. We might say the latter group was born with talent.

If we bring the argument into a systems context for a group of humans, those of us who coach teams have no doubt that leadership can be developed spectacularly. We live it every day. Experience shows us that the key point is not just that the leader figure is present, but rather that leadership potential exists within the group. Within the group there really are people able to demonstrate leadership in the right moment. And the path to achieving this state lies in the leader being a true maker of leaders, a sower of leadership. For me, this is another excellent indicator that the quality of leadership is clearly linked to the presence of those two qualities we mentioned above: humility and generosity.

If you lead a department or an organization, would you rather have just one engine—yourself—or several synergistic ones? The vast majority of professionals seem to prefer the latter but how many of them practice it? Now we're back to running into our ego: If I think that leadership is my property, I won't give others the tools to take it from me! I will have put myself on a path to becoming not a leader, but an autocrat. In reality, a high-quality leader is a maker of leaders, whereas mediocre leaders see other potential leaders as threats and cut down their development path.

Let this also help clarify something important: Not only can a leader be made, he can also be unmade. If you become disconnected from the team or their trust, it will cost you your leadership. Therefore, leadership is made, learned, and developed. It also has to be cared for, watered, and nurtured relentlessly.

The 21st-Century Scientist and the Shaman

In the industrial revolution, humans slowly made the transition from craftsmen, the owners who were solely responsible for their work, to operators bolted to a production process that they cannot fully see, one that is vastly larger than them, and that they rarely even understand. For this reason, they don't feel like it belongs to them. Technological change leads to a world in which human beings are at the same level as machines, if not lower: a labor pool, a workforce, or human resources.

People effectively become resources, often as easy to trade as stock, depending on the profitability, or the politics, involved. It's a world of fire and metal: rough, composed of pieces, machinery, systems, and factories that each morning swallow up thousands of men and women to spit them back out at the end of the day, empty and exhausted. In return it provides material progress the likes of which have never been seen before. Science and knowledge grow to limits previously unthinkable. Today we have more toys than ever and they're more dispensable than ever. We are children of this period in history.

Since the enlightenment, that world has been feeding us an apparent rationality in which logic, science, and engineering reign in our companies while emotional factors like hope and fear—and, naturally, magic—have all but disappeared. We have been, and are, presumably rational people—as we have been taught to be—who don't take into account the real human engine that, whether we accept it or not, inhabits the emotional part of our brain. It is precisely there that leadership's potential for invigorating others lies.

And yet, from the shadows those powerful emotional factors have continued to carry out their voiceless work. Of course, we have had to learn to identify them by reading between the lines: Through the deafening noise of workshops and the cold sterility of offices, in that rewarding and ruthless real world where real people live. They have hidden themselves from view in that corporate office life with its graphs, spreadsheets, carpets, and overly trendy wardrobes.

Fortunately, advances in science are showing us how human beings really operate through greater understanding of the human brain. After the 1990s, various researchers started to take giant steps in this area. Technology allowed us to observe the brain in action and Daniel Goleman combined these findings into a single general focus under the label emotional intelligence.

That which doesn't have a name, doesn't exist. In certain indigenous tribes of the Americas, traitors were punished by being stripped of their names. They usually wound up dying in solitude. Now, thanks to the concept of emotional intelligence, the emotional nature of man has a name and the world is starting to respond to its influence.

Human beings are beginning to be seen in their entirety and not just as parts of an erector set. This new concept has given the world, and particularly the business world, quite a shock to the system. That world is just now beginning to reconcile itself with our true nature. This is, and will continue to be, a fascinating time filled with uncertainty. We will uncover things that previously would have been unimaginable. I wouldn't trade it for anything!

Quantum physics and electronics provide new approaches to researching and measuring, albeit awkwardly at first, that human factor. And they provide powerful theoretical analogies that cast a new light over how we function individually and as a community. A basic example is the interpretation of human groups using systems theory, which is widely applied in team coaching. We are living the remarkable process of reconciliation between that rational man and the previously unseen, new-ancestral emotional man that we are just discovering. How lucky are we to be a part of this process? And wouldn't it be better to actively participate in the process rather than to be a mere spectator?

Is the 21st-century scientist on his way to being reintroduced to the shaman?

Well, this reconciliation process is forcing us to rethink those dominant Taylorist schemes and to regain a craftsman, even medieval, spirit, as Irish author and professor Charles Handy proposed, in which man once again has dominion over his work and is proud of what he does. A world in which work once again has meaning and fills us with pride for what we do!

Without even knowing it, we're revisiting ancient ways of looking at life. These ways have been dormant and we desperately need them if we are to re-establish our relationship with nature and the transcendent—a relationship shaken by tremendous development in science. A kind of planetary consciousness is starting to stumble into view and, along with it, a sense that we are all connected. Lack of this consciousness sparks systemic imbalances in which a small group can cause problems that will take millions of people a long time to resolve. For examples of this we can point to nuclear accidents like the one at Chernobyl or a financial crisis of staggering proportions. May the shaman's wisdom come to our aid!

We Are What We Believe

We're not quick to learn when what we learn causes us to modify our mental schemes, our structure, or belief system. Beliefs are to our thoughts what our skeleton is to our body: They are the source code of the thoughts we generate and the tools we use to face what comes our way in life. It is much easier to change the machines and processes than the combination of values and beliefs—what we call corporate culture—of an organization or a country. Later, we will stop for a moment to look at how beliefs work. For now, we'll just say that this is where change processes tend to fail and where resistance to them starts.

It's normal to be afraid! Things are happening that have never happened before and we lack the mental resources to understand them. That's why the world that we're coming into begs for growth, both personal and professional —deep down there is no difference.

I remember when Spain adopted the Euro as a currency. I was talking to my grandmother, who at the time was well into her 90s and was bothered by the fact that she couldn't get the hang of these "new *pesetas.*" Trying to cheer her up, I argued that she was well accustomed to change and I started reminding her of all of the major changes that she had already lived through. But as I did this, I started to scare myself: the Internet, mobile phones, and television. The airplane! The automobile! Wow! I mean, she was born in 1907!

I realized that I was part of an experimental generation to whom the major changes that my grandmother had lived through would seem small, and that these would, in turn, seem ridiculous to the next generation. I suddenly became aware that the cultural and educational resources that I had at my disposal didn't evolve fast enough to face this change and that this would cause a great deal of uncertainty. I lacked references. Unbelievable things were happening every day. My belief system was going to need a complete overhaul!

The changes we live through are not without pain and trauma. In fact, the more we resist, the more pain we will feel. As psychiatrist Carl Gustav Jung said, "what you resist, persists and what you accept, changes." Acceptance, and thus the ability to change, requires learning to modify our beliefs and find inner strength because change also brings fear, uncertainty, and sometimes even a bit of vertigo.

> We aren't taught to modify our beliefs, which makes sense. Human life has traditionally been quite short and it has developed in a stable cultural and technological context. So beliefs were always forever.

For example, the life of a medieval peasant was very similar to that of his father and grandfather. He would encounter the same dangers and the same circumstances. For him, the experience was a paradigm of the highest value. Life's uncertainties were basic, brutal, and clear (for instance, "if we have a bad harvest, will I survive the next winter?"). In contrast, today, especially in the West, we're not excessively worried about surviving the winter, but we are worried about getting a job or paying a mortgage. We also suffer from information overload: We process more information in one week than our medieval peasant friend would in his entire life. That creates a level of stress of a new and different nature.

We are facing new problems with expired belief systems. We are not prepared or trained to modify them. We live in a state of heightened uncertainty that makes us insecure and awakens a wide variety of fears, defensiveness, selfishness, and toxic behavior.

This is the reason that leadership is so fashionable today! We need leadership to face the uncertainty: It's the resource that we humans have to confront the unknown, to find the path amid the fog, and to give the best of ourselves as we take each step, even if it doesn't always turn out how we had hoped. In what other time was the uncertainty of change greater? When has the fog of things to come been denser than it is today?

Luckily, we have tools and techniques to deal with those fears and decide how we want to live out a certain situation. Some of those techniques come from recent advances in neuroscience, but others are ancient and we are just now rediscovering them. Such as, for example, family constellations.

If you see leadership as a path full of effort and personal growth, demanding but also rewarding, you're off to a good start. And if at any time things don't turn out as you had hoped, remember that this was your idea. Don't panic. Like in any other path of personal growth, stumbling is a part of progress. It doesn't matter that you fall down, just that you get back up. How exciting to build this future!

Welcome to the world of leadership!

2

Emotion and Leadership

Although traditional incentives such as bonuses or recognition can prod people to better performance, no external motivators can get people to perform at their absolute best.

—Goleman, Boyatzis, and McKee (2003)

In the Beginning, There Was Emotion

As we saw in the previous chapter, leadership is a means for groups of humans to survive. But how does it work? To understand it we have to start by uncovering the mechanism of emotional response. Have you ever wondered why you have emotions? What good are they? Why haven't humans evolved into perfect rational beings like Mr. Spock, the Vulcan from *Star Trek*? They probably tried that on you in school, explaining that reason was our most important quality.

The truth is that the most rational part of the brain—specifically the prefrontal cortex—is too limited to decide everything in our lives. It's a relative newcomer to the brain compared with other, older areas like the limbic system, our emotional manager, or the instinctive brain, sometimes called the lizard brain, which dates back to the age of the dinosaurs. But we reserve our rational brain for certain activities because it would be limited in others.

Can you imagine deciding which shoe to put on first every morning on the basis of rational analysis?

We never would have made it as a species that way! To give you some reference, your brain manages 11,000 mental processes a minute. Of those, only 50 are done consciously! The bulk of our lives takes place in the subconscious.

We use shortcuts like habit to streamline our decision-making processes. We also use emotions, which make us predisposed to favor certain options that we sense or want more; this also becomes a shortcut that accelerates the decision-making process.

Maybe you've already heard the news: It has been scientifically proven that human beings are not rational beings, contrary to what they would have had us believe in school. In 1994, neurologist Antonio Damasio laid out in his book, *Descartes' Error*, a somatic marker hypothesis. In it, he proposed that human beings are not rational beings, but rather beings that rationalize over an emotional base that ultimately conditions how they will think. That is to say that first we feel, and then we think.

So from inception, our brain's response to environmental stimuli immediately mixes emotions and thoughts in the vast majority of situations. For example, solving a simple math problem is not likely to evoke an emotional response. But if you're the slightest bit under the gun or if the process seems somewhat tedious, your brain functions start to change, increasing the chances that you'll make a mistake. In practice this means that our focus on being objective will never be more than a utopic myth—except maybe for Mr. Spock.

> We are evolutionarily designed to be eminently emotional beings.
> For that reason, if we want to continue progressing, we will need to
> understand what emotions and feelings are, as well as how they function.

So let's take a look: If you were to suddenly find yourself in front of a lion, your senses would send nerve impulses to a structure of the brain called the amygdala—a term that comes from the Greek word for almond after its shape—located in the part of the brain known as the limbic system. Your amygdala would undergo a process of rapid data checking against its archive—memory is located in the same part of the brain—to confirm the potential threat. Then it would send nerve signals to another part of the brain, the motor cortex, to activate movement of the extremities. And at the same time, it would unleash a cascade of hormones resulting in the secretion of adrenaline, which prepares your metabolic furnace to feed your muscles the energy they need to carry out the enormous task of saving your life. In layman's terms, that lion gave you quite a scare. That scare is just an emotion, a marvelous physiological vortex brought to you by millions of years of evolution!

So What Is a Feeling?

As we have seen, our brain doesn't accurately distinguish a rational thought from the preceding emotion that conditions it (and sometimes even causes it). When we experience an intense emotion, we can make ourselves aware of it and even give it a name, for instance, fear in the lion scenario. This realization then triggers a chain of thoughts—an internal dialogue commonly called driving yourself crazy—that are rooted in our belief system and mental framework. Keeping with the lion example, the process could go something like this:

"I'm scared. Men shouldn't be scared. I am a warrior and I cannot be afraid but I am. I am a coward. My father was right." And so on!

This emotion, combined with the awareness that we are having the emotion, plus all of the mental unraveling that follows, constitutes a feeling. From inception it has a basis in a purely physiological response that triggers a highly complex mental construction about the situation. All of this comes together to make up what we now refer to as the emotional impact that the situation has provoked.

For this reason, humans are incapable of experiencing reality through our feelings. Basically, we cannot separate an event from its emotional impact on us. Thus, what we call reality is actually perception! The good news is that by recognizing the mechanism—since avoidance of an automatic response is impossible—we can manage it.

Emotional Management and Leadership

We have a biological tendency to be led by our emotions, which leads us to three mechanisms of innate response. These avoidance behaviors are well studied and defined. They are named after their objective of survival by avoiding the threat:

- Flight is the preferred option in terms of cost-benefit ratio when faced with a threat. Or, in its modern form, disconnecting, like what happens when we pretend to be listening while someone reprimands us, but we are actually thinking about our vacation plans.

- Fight means physical confrontation, which in its more common form refers to mouthing off.

- Freezing up is when we make ourselves stiff as a statue so that our predator won't notice us. This is sometimes represented by being left speechless.

These mechanisms are profoundly ingrained in our biology, as is typical of many mammals. They are also very powerful, as we can see when we witness a group in panic. You're probably alive today and reading these pages because at some moment in your life one of these mechanisms forced you to get out of the way of a speeding car before getting flattened. Or it helped you stand up to a bully in school—or to run from him. Or to stand there and get screamed at by an angry dictatorial boss. The evolution of our species has caused a steady increase in the complexity of the situations we face. So response mechanisms as simple and direct as these gradually become more and more inadequate and inefficient.

Imagine, for example, that you are a salesperson. You are dealing with a particularly disrespectful client who screams, "you and your company think you're pulling one over on me and I am sick of you!" An outright and direct attack! You, like the good mammal that you are, walk over to the client and slap him in the face several times for being so unbearable. "He deserved it and it felt great," you later tell your boss as you collect your things from your desk and are escorted out of the building. What if instead, without saying a word, you broke into a full sprint and didn't stop until you were down the block? Or if you were left speechless in the presence of this predator?

In an earlier phase of my career I trained more than 2,000 business-people from various companies and sectors. I can assure you that any expert salesperson knows that flight, fight, and freeze will not help. Yet, many people settle for controlling their impulses, suppressing their biological response, and paying the price of swallowing the enormous inner tension that this causes. This is then released when we least expect it or it affects our health in the form of stress, a phenomenon unique to mammals and extensively studied by biologists like Robert Sapolsky, professor at Stanford University.

In situations of stress, the body is saturated with the hormone cortisol, which is designed to help the body survive situations of prolonged stress (from the perspective of a hominid millions of years ago). It's an adequate mechanism to confront the fear of going on a hunt in a predator-filled forest and to face the uncertainty of having to either hunt or starve. But not to be tactful with a client.

Cortisol changes our body's priorities. It sacrifices certain long-term capabilities, such as the immune system or sex drive, for the sake of other short-term ones that focus on getting maximum efficiency in the avoidance behaviors fight, flight, and freezing up. In the brain, cortisol promotes certain avoidance behavior, while suppressing those centers that stimulate creativity, learning, and identifying opportunities. As a result, your brain behaves in a way more similar to a primitive mammal and will not be able to find creative and effective solutions, or come up with innovative ways to face a situation. In layman's terms, you'll be in a fog.

> We confirm again that life puts us in many situations for which our default biological responses are inadequate!

In contrast, to succeed with that angry client, you will need to know how to relativize the situation, put it into context, realize how it affects you, regain your composure, be able to listen and ask questions to find out what's behind that attack, and, lastly, know how to identify opportunities that will undoubtedly emerge from the storm. You will have to learn to manage yourself in order to manage others. You should know how to go beyond simply controlling your impulses. Control alone will engulf you in cortisol. You need a clear mind in order to:

- Be aware of the emotion you are having or, put another way, be able to realize how you are living the situation.

- Accept that emotion, be open to it, listen to it. That way you can realize the emotional impact it has had on you.

- Gain insight and understanding about that impact.

- From that understanding, keep a calm and open mind to imagine possible new approaches to the situation. Identify opportunities, ways out, or even how to turn the situation to your advantage.

- Focus on being constructive and positive in order to act decisively and energetically.

It is very important to keep in mind that, just as the three avoidance behaviors we described are innate, this process of true self-management requires training. The good news is that learning it is within the reach of all humans that have a normal brain, by which I mean one that's not pathological. But knowing this loads us with the weight of responsibility: If we don't do it, it's because we don't want to. Complaining is not allowed!

So what does this explanation have to do with leadership?

Long ago the ultimate goal of a leadership relationship was to get the most out of the group's abilities to ensure their survival; today it is to help the group achieve their goals. And let's remember that the group chooses the person that it feels can best trigger this process as the leader.

As a result, a person capable of self-management will be better suited to find solutions to the group's situation and encourage others to do the same. This is usually referred to as the capacity to lead oneself, personal leadership, or self-leadership.

Consider this for a moment: In a difficult situation, whom would you give leadership to? Whom would you look to? Probably the person most capable of thinking clearly. Isn't leadership incredibly important for the human group? The leader is the catalyzer for the group's resources: She makes things possible, or better, and makes things happen because people want to do them and feel like they can. But in order to do that she must first demonstrate good self-management or personal leadership.

Managing Emotion and Managing Relationships

Seeing the leader as the catalyzer brings us to something important—understanding that the leader doesn't have to personally possess the resources the team requires. His true function is to make the resources, be they mental or physical, flow between the members of the group. It is possible, and, in fact, common, for those resources to belong to other members of the group who do not have the option to lead.

There is a film, based on the novel by British author Elleston Trevor, that discusses this very clearly. The film is *Flight of the Phoenix* and there have been two versions: the first directed by Robert Aldrich in 1965 and the second by John Moore in 2004. Time periods and special effects aside, they both tell almost the exact same story, although they take place in different locations. In the 2004 remake, a group of oil workers flying to the Gobi Desert are hit by a sandstorm, have to travel way off their route, and are forced to crash land in the middle of nowhere. Their plane is badly damaged and their resources dwindle quickly.

When they realize they will not be rescued, they have to find a way out of their situation before they run out of water. I won't spoil the ending for you, although, it being a Hollywood feature, you would expect it to end well. I will say that the group starts to act like a team only when the leader, the plane's pilot, manages to communicate effectively with one of the passengers, an engineer who has the knowledge they need but completely lacks social skills and doesn't get along with anyone. The leader does not have the resources, in this case knowledge, but he gets the rest of the group to listen to the one person who does have them, despite their resistance.

This function of leadership is increasingly important in a world growing increasingly more complex, especially one that has too much partial or fragmented information. It is impossible to have all the information that exists, so we need greater cooperation between individuals, especially when working within a network. In the past, structuring teams mechanically was good enough. Tasks could be put together like an assembly line—the operating points were clear and the friction points between those in charge were clear too.

In a complex world, in a context of increasingly accelerating change, members of a team must not only rethink how to complete tasks, but also how to review the procedures cooperatively and contribute their ideas to that review. They must also participate in constant adjustment of the team's mission, vision, and values.

In fact, success depends more and more on external collaborators located in the team's gray zones: people partially integrated into the team in certain phases of a particular project who, not being formally part of the team, should contribute the same energy as those core members, and over whom the leader tends to lack formal authority. Leadership is almost more important with this group. And especially in three concrete aspects:

- The inspirational aspect that drives everyone to commit to the project, whatever the contractual or official status.

- The relationship aspect contributes to the creation and care of relationships that foster cooperation. This is very reminiscent of the affiliate leadership proposed by Goleman, Boyatzis, and McKee in *Primal Leadership* (2002).

- Most important of all is the leader as maker of leaders, who encourages leaders to flourish through the entire organization. A leader must become a diffuser of leadership and a genuine teacher of it.

The act of working within a network poses a very interesting point: Leading by the old paradigm—focusing on just one person—could hinder the development of the group! Deborah Ancona, director of the MIT Leadership Center, summarizes it loud and clear:

> The myth of the omniscient, omnipotent leader is causing more harm than good because it ultimately erodes peoples' confidence. Those who try to do everything themselves will be defeated by a world that is increasingly complex and unpredictable. In truth, we are all incomplete leaders who must rely on others. The challenge is to develop the mechanisms that allow us to pull on the ideas and motivations of

> creative minds throughout the organization, to leverage the strengths of the group, and to think about networks of leaders working together to move the organization ahead. (Watt 2012)

To achieve what Ancona proposes, a leader must, on the one hand, have a deep understanding of the current environment and, on the other, be able to manage his own emotions to cultivate the two key values that we already know: humility and generosity. Only in this way can he distance himself from the patrimonial and limiting vision of leadership and allow the three key aspects we've already discussed to flourish.

That's the reason that effective leadership development programs start with self-leadership first. Without fail, improving personal leadership—I lead myself through self-leadership—changes the influence we have on others, enhancing our outward leadership.

Want to improve your leadership? Start by knowing yourself better. Accept your emotional side and give it permission to help you!

3

Leadership From Within

A British corporal described General Slim talking to his unit:

> There were no exhortations or grandiose clichés; there were no jokes
> or barracks talk. . . . Informally, he told us what would happen, in the
> reflective tone of an intimate conversation. And we believed everything
> he said, carried out every order. I think his greatest gift was an ability
> to create a sense of being close to us, as though he were chatting offhand
> to an understanding nephew. . . . He had the head of a general with the
> heart of a private soldier. (Stouffer 1949, quoted in Burleigh 2010)

We have seen that leadership is really a type of relationship. For that
reason, as in all human relationships, creating a leadership relationship
requires that not just the aspiring leader, but also the other members of the
human group, want to create it, share it, and nurture it. That is:

1. to feel that the leadership candidate is someone worthy of being
    heard and worth believing in

2. the candidate proposes things you care about.

In that order! In other words, however important you think what you are
proposing may be for the team, you will never generate a leadership relationship without first establishing a base of trust. If you have that trust, what you
say will not be valued in the same way as if you didn't. The question, then, is
how do you create that trust?

Obviously, there is a trust that comes from shared experience, if they have seen you act in similar situations and the group has gotten a good feeling from them, that would be considered worthy of trust. You would have achieved an a posteriori trust. Notice that however unfair it may seem trust will be based more on the emotional residue that the acts left behind, than on the objective acts themselves.

In management, we often see ourselves in situations that require the trust of the group without having been able to gain it through shared experience. This is very common, for example, when:

- The group doesn't really know you because you're new to the team and, despite this, your bosses are already expecting miracles.

- The group perceives the situation as something completely new to you and feels that prior experience is meaningless.

- Your role has changed recently and you haven't yet been accepted by the organization. For example, after a recent promotion, your old colleagues still view you as a peer.

In these situations we need another type of trust, referred to as a priori, and that, unlike the previous type, should come from expectations we should be able to create.

OK, so how do I go about gaining a priori trust?

A priori trust comes from your ability to create and communicate believable expectations that minimize uncertainty. For people to do things, we first have to want to do them (attitude) and even before that, we have to believe that they're possible—or better still, desirable. Otherwise, we will not move or allow ourselves to be moved easily!

"Yes, we can!" The motto that drove Barack Obama to the White House was hope! Hope is incredibly powerful and can be used to motivate and demotivate. It's a secret weapon of leadership and an essential result of positive expectations. We will discuss how to create positive expectations later.

Imagine you have hope readily available. How will you get them to buy into it? Let's look at an example.

Who Hasn't Had This Happen to Them?

Here is a very common, real-life situation for any middle manager: You receive instructions to take charge of a team that faces some complicated task with very few resources and you decide on a course of action that you have trouble understanding clearly. Being the good professional, you take on the challenge responsibly and in good spirits. You are ready to make use of the communication techniques the company has given you in the workshops they've been organizing. You prepare yourself and carefully construct your message, but you can't get completely comfortable with it, even though you know it's what you have to say. You arm yourself with courage and go at it with energy and vigor.

To your surprise, the team is immediately defensive. They aggressively focus on the difficulties and only half listen to the goodies that you have so ably offered them. "That's strange. They don't usually do this," you tell yourself. It's as if they could smell the doubt you were holding back.

You start to feel insincere and realize you're achieving the opposite of what you wanted. This is not going well. Quick! Do something! With your trademark vigor, you spring back and end up righting the ship by, as you would put it, "cutting the crap." You quickly rifle off a series of instructions that immediately gets everyone into gear. You are not achieving leadership. You are acting like a boss: You have gotten them working, but not wanting to work.

Later, when you've calmed down, you reflect—some managers still do this—and you realize that your team read every internal doubt you were trying to keep from them. You realize that if you do not believe in what you do, your team will pick up on it to the point where you may get the opposite of what you were looking for. Emotions travel at incredible speeds between individuals through nonverbal communication, which, according to some experts, accounts for 80 percent of all communication.

So it seems that in order to lead, you either do what you believe in or you learn to believe in what you're doing. In other words, to lead a project, you either believe in it outright or you find new ways of seeing it that allow you to believe in it. Finding these perspectives is fundamental to creating the key element of leadership that we call vision. We will comment on this extensively later.

> If you manage to create new approaches that you can believe in, you will have the opportunity to transmit them to the team and then you will have something to say that makes you feel genuine.

The wonderful thing is that there are already techniques to help you develop this internal coherence. This is one of the principal reasons for the coaching boom in organizations. It will improve your ability to convince and inspire, your team will notice it, and the chances of them following you, of them wanting to do, will be infinitely greater.

The process of building trust, starting from the end result and working back to the cause, will be the following:

1. The a priori trust you achieve will come from your credibility.

2. Your credibility will depend on your authenticity, which is a perception that you should inspire in the members of the group.

3. Authenticity will come from the sense that you are a complete person, someone who says what he does and does what he says.

4. This perception will be decisively marked by your nonverbal communication, which will depend largely on the involuntary gestures that are controlled by the subconscious.

5. Involuntary gestures transmit your real attitude toward what you are saying. If you don't believe in it, people will notice a dissonance

between your emotions and your actions. They will become distrustful and go on the defensive. They probably won't know exactly why, but that won't matter.

In summary, you can either be a great actor—only the best actors can communicate emotions they don't feel—or you had better work on truly feeling what you say. For that, leadership will demand of you an intense personal feat to harmonize your vision of how things should be with how things are—that which we inaccurately call reality, and which in reality is just a perception. That effort is what Peter Senge refers to as creative tension. It makes leadership into a journey of personal and professional development that is rooted in self-awareness and delving into human nature.

Developing leadership places the task of knowing yourself and others squarely in your lap. It requires a sustained effort of resisting self-deception and being humble enough to accept failure. For that reason, good leaders are scarce. It is much easier to be a good boss—giving orders allows you to change others without having to change yourself, at least, at first.

In fact, in his book *The Fifth Discipline* (1990), when Peter Senge discusses the discipline of personal mastery, he indicates that people who have highly developed it share certain characteristics:

- Their vision is vocation.
- They see actual reality as an ally and have learned to work with the forces of change rather than against them.
- They want to be more aware of reality.
- They feel connected with others and with life without sacrificing their personality.
- They feel like part of a broader creative process in which they can influence without controlling.
- They live in constant apprenticeship: Personal mastery is not a characteristic you possess, but rather a lifelong process that involves being aware of your weaknesses or areas of growth. In

other words, we would say that they are people capable of leaving their comfort zone and feeling the satisfaction of doing so, because for them the reward is worth the trip.

- They look intensely for emotional learning.
- They love their work. For them, work is not just a way of earning money.
- They focus on relevant, not secondary, objectives.

Aren't all of these characteristics requirements for leadership?

Rational thought is great for creating action plans, not energizing people. Earlier, we cited the famous speech—considered one of the most important of the 20th century—given by Martin Luther King Jr., on August 28, 1963, from the steps of the Lincoln Memorial in Washington, D.C. King said "I have a dream," not "let's work toward a reasonable reduction in racism in the United States of around 8.7 percent this year."

Getting people to want to move requires them to feel what they're doing. This means first creating a shared emotional foundation between the leader and the led, one based on trust, from which you can build that communal sense. That will not be possible if they do not see the living embodiment of their project in their leader. This condition is not suggested; it is required. In short, if you want to lead a project, first you should live it intensely.

What will happen if I do that and do not achieve the commitment I want?

You will probably feel frustrated and your ego will flare up. Ego is a piece of software designed to facilitate your survival as an individual. To that end, it will call on your resources to protect your self-esteem, which you need to get ahead. As a consequence, it will also trigger magnificent processes of self-deception designed to justify your decisions and actions and, if necessary, to cast blame on others.

It's easy to assume that these processes reduce your capacity for objectivity and empathy, which seriously influence your leadership. The ego's power will create a polarized perception: You will become convinced of convenient "truths" about your position and about the incompetence, or even the malice, of others. It will make you feel as though you were looking at the world through deformed glasses. Your connection to the team will suffer and it could even end up being disconnected entirely. If that happens, your capacity for leadership will be null and the team will put their trust in someone else. Period.

Now, in that moment you will still have the power. You can be what we call a boss. Consequently, this risk increases if you take on both roles simultaneously: the role of power (the boss) and the role of authority (leadership). If your position is that of informal leader—without hierarchical power—you will not experience the temptation that this implies for your ego.

Essentially, the ego starts an internal dialogue to salvage your self-esteem, which could take several forms: "they don't deserve me," "they're stupid," or even "this is a conspiracy." All of this is normal! You can learn a lot from properly managing that frustration. And to do that you need to cultivate two values that are critical to good leadership and which we have previously mentioned: humility and generosity.

So, I can only avoid that danger by succeeding?

Also incorrect! Success brings satisfaction and that also awakens the ego in a way that starts a process, which, if you aren't lucky enough to occasionally fail in a big way, will make you feel invincible. This is what famous soccer coach Josep Guardiola calls "having a fit of self-importance."

The end result will be a belief that "I am the team," or worse "I know what's best for them more than they do." Doubtlessly, others will take note and over time you will lose the emotional connection, causing them to pass their trust onto another leader. If you have power, you can prevent this by force and end up a dictator. Thus this path also requires humility and generosity.

That's one heck of a challenge!

Attaining leadership is hard work and so is keeping it. Being a leader means living what you do, but not depending on it! Personal leadership marries poorly with relationships that are dependent upon people or things.

In reality, we only possess that which we are willing to let go of. If you cannot let go of something that thing owns you instead! If you have a nice car, but you're constantly worried about someone scratching it, the reality is that you are your vehicle's property.

Ask yourself this question honestly: If you are given some level of responsibility in an organization and do not feel genuine regarding what you have to do or say, could you give it up? If the answer is yes, you own that position. If the answer is no, that position owns you. You will be dependent on it and will live with the permanent risk of doing things that go against what your professional criteria dictate, acting on your political conveniences to maintain your position. Don't worry. Your ego will supply you with an ample repertoire of justifications—we never seem to run out of those—to calm you, at least on the surface. However, you will lose authenticity—and as a result authority—and your leadership will suffer.

But there's always hope: find within yourself new perspectives about what you do (and how you do it) that will let you sincerely believe in, and reconnect with, your work to continue to be authentic.

And we're almost at the finish line!

An Overview of
Systems Thinking

When I started coaching, Dick Motta, a veteran NBA coach, told me that the most important part of the job takes place on the practice floor, not during the game. After a certain point you have to trust in the players to translate into action what they've learned in practice. . . . Once the players have mastered the system, a powerful group intelligence emerges that is greater than the coach's ideas or those of any individual on the team. When a team reaches that state, the coach can step back and let the game itself "motivate" the players.

—Phil Jackson, *Sacred Hoops*

What Is a System?

This chapter will provide an overview of systems thinking. We have seen that the leader plays a role in the system, but what do we mean by system? It can be defined as an entity made up of certain elements plus the relationships that exist between them. The elements create relationships to achieve a common purpose and are interconnected in such a way that a change in any one of them inevitably affects them all. They behave differently as part of the system than they would if they were independent.

For example, let's take the simplest human system: the couple. If you pay close attention to a couple, you will see that neither one of them acts exactly the same when they are together as when they are apart. In fact, you can apply the same coaching process to that entity, the couple, as you would to a person, using modified techniques, of course. Tribes, departments in a company, or sports teams are other examples of systems. They are entities that once configured take on a life of their own beyond the individuals that make them up—sometimes surprisingly so!

> Managing a team of people from a systems perspective requires starting with a group vision and focusing closely on the established relationships between the elements that make up the system, then working on these relationships to influence the operation of the whole system.

To achieve a systemic vision of the group you have to avoid any mechanical perspectives that view the organization as a structure made up of pieces to be assembled that operate mechanically, like an engine. Instead, you should work toward a fluid vision, one composed of currents of information and energy.

Mechanical visions have long dominated the analysis and structuring of organizations. This is because relationships between the elements tend to be obscured, even confusing, and, until now, difficult to measure. Our mentality, often reinforced by the overly technical and scientific education of managers—as was the case with me—has made us focus on the tangible: the pieces of the machine. The result is that we adopt decisions that are logical from a mechanical perspective, but incorrect from a systemic perspective, resulting in decisions that have negative consequences on the evolution of the team. The fact that something is intangible doesn't mean it doesn't exist, just that we lack the instruments we need to measure it. Fortunately, we are finding methods to make the intangible tangible, which allow us to measure characteristics that are critical to the performance and evolution of a team.

I learned the limitations of my mechanical vision of organizations through experience—which in this case means through making mistakes—first as a manager and later as a consultant. It was probably this discovery that led me to coaching teams. As a consultant, I dedicated a lot of time to diagnostics and designing a corresponding action plan. My clients would then implement the plan, investing their time and money. And then the plan often did not work! Or it partially worked, but fell short of the agreed-upon terms. I couldn't figure it out! It frustrated me to no end.

If you have ever been in charge of projects, the same thing has probably happened to you. Intelligent people design a logical plan. They communicate it clearly to the people implementing it, a group of highly trained professionals, but after all that, it doesn't work! What goes wrong? Where do these projects fall apart? Looking for answers, I saw that in most cases the problems stemmed from emotions and relationships.

People do not resist change, but rather being changed! Uncertainty inspires fear, resistance, and toxic behavior. Without solid leadership, you get cliques, gangs, and other problems. Uncertainty takes over people's hearts and their actions stray from logic.

Let's take a real-life example from a few years ago: In the Spanish headquarters of a multinational consumer electronics company, leaders wished to implement a customer relationship management system to optimize client management. The salespeople were trained properly and shown the advantages of the system, as well as how much time it would save them. They seemed to welcome the new system, but as time passed they hardly ever used it. Did they understand all the benefits? Perfectly! They are intelligent people and have been well trained. So, what's the problem? There was a leadership problem; the sales team did not fully trust their managers and feared that the real reason for this new system was to gain more control over them. So they approached it with suspicion. The problem was not the salespeople. It is the relationship they had with their theoretical leaders! In the context of a more trusting system, these problems would not have appeared.

The System Revelation

Everything starts with a very important first step; it is common for members of a system to be unaware that they are part of it. When we work with a team to apply systemic coaching techniques, it is essential to cause the system revelation, that is:

- The system becomes aware of itself, that it is something communal of which everyone is a part. It is an entity that acts as if it were a single individual. Any member of a system will behave differently within it than outside it.

- The system must accept itself and how it actually works: its priorities, its tendencies, its likes, and dislikes. When a system accepts itself, it is able to say, "Okay, this is we act. Now we can decide how we want to act from here on out." Again, we are reminded of psychologist Carl Jung, who said, "what you resist, persists and what you accept, changes." Later we will see in greater detail how, from this acceptance, the system can start to define itself and how it will deal with change.

The sooner this revelation happens, the better for the system. This level of consciousness is usually only achieved spontaneously, if it is achieved at all, when circumstances push us into it, like in times of crisis, and by that time it is too late to find solutions. "We were at the edge of the abyss, but fortunately we were able to take a step forward," is an old business owner's joke.

And at this point the presence of group leadership is crucial; the leader's role in the system is fundamental to promoting the revelation of the system. When a leader has the capacity—by training or intuition—to understand the system, she opens the door for others to also become aware of it. As change accelerates and complexity grows, it increases the need for systems to evolve.

And since that ability depends on the previous revelation, it means that leadership will increasingly demand more relational consciousness and a better systemic view. In fact, a leader must have that systemic awareness in order to succeed in the process that we call having vision, which we will discuss more later.

Feedback and Homeostasis

Systems always tend to maintain their balance. This is the principle of homeostasis—from the Greek *homo*, meaning similar, and *estasis*, meaning position. What it means in practice is that left alone, the system always finds a way to maintain balance and avoid change.

Relationships that are established between system elements are determined by feedback processes. They are referred to this way because part of the initial impulse—the output of the system—is fed back into the system as information about said output. Two types of feedback exist:

- Positive feedback confirms that the system's initial impulse—the output—is correct, causing the maintenance or increase of said initial output. Therefore, information amplifies that impulse, triggering a variation in the system.

- Negative feedback is characterized as such because, in contrast to its counterpart, it uses information that was fed back to the system to change the initial impulse, deactivating the variation.

Closed systems are those that are disconnected from their environment. Homeostasis in these systems is normal. In contrast, open systems are those that interact with their surroundings. In closed systems, changes are produced within the internal relationships, whereas in open systems there is always a possibility that the system itself will change. In this sense, human relationships tend to be open systems.

Are Some Systems Selfish?

The answer seems to be a clear and definitive "yes." People are often relatively or completely unaware of how their actions affect the rest of the system. They are as unaware of this as they are of how the actions of others can affect them. We have seen that in revealing the system to itself, you increase the level of awareness in a way that helps the system redesign itself. However, when the level of awareness is low, it is very common for certain elements to cause imbalances within the system for their own gain. They are sure that they can emerge unscathed only to find that they are dragged through the whirlwind they have created. I write these lines in the midst of an economic crisis that has been called a systemic crisis. Is it any wonder why?

In an increasingly interconnected world, the actions of a few have a greater impact on the rest of the population; selfish intentions are more and more costly to others, even if the culprits go unpunished. This type of behavior is more destructive to the system the greater its complexity and interconnection, and could eventually lead to the collapse of the system. The same happens, albeit in reverse, with actions that push the system to evolve toward a more efficient way of achieving its goal. For this point, the influence of leadership is key. Without it, the process is entirely impossible. In fact, here we stumble upon a very interesting point: What separates a leader from a manipulator?

From the system's perspective, a leader works toward evolving the system, or in other words, works for the group, not for himself. A manipulator uses the same techniques as a leader, but works toward his own ends, motivated by what we earlier called systemic selfishness. A manipulator and a leader both use their influence on an emotional level and can even use the same techniques, but with differences in the intention and conscience; a leader works for the collective, while a manipulator works for himself. The manipulator isn't the least bit concerned with the consequences that his actions have on others. The manipulator is not genuine and his apparent authority will breed resentment, although any good manipulator can fool you long enough to achieve her goals.

If you wish to be a good manipulator, it's in your best interest to abide by the "take the money and run" strategy: Embed yourself, identify weaknesses, make decisions, buy support, eliminate your obstacles, reap the rewards, and move along to milk another system before the consequences can catch up with you.

What Should a Leader Do?

We've seen that the leader should contribute to the system's revelation and then help it evolve. For that you need a dual perspective, including vision from both the ground level and a bird's eye view.

- **Vision from the trenches:** Descend into the battleground and get yourself into the mud. That means sharing in the team's circumstances—the disappointments and the joys of their work. You need to stay close and know how they live firsthand, not by what others tell you. This is reminiscent of what Tom Peters proposed in the 1980s as "itinerant leadership."

- **Vision from command central:** You should know how to see the battleground as a whole, and have a general view of the system and its context, without being blinded by planning and analyzing partial aspects, however much they may call your attention.

Combining both perspectives will give you the insight you need to create and illuminate a vision for your team. We have already seen that a leader is a manager of uncertainty. Your objective is to reduce it so that people are confident enough to take on a constructive attitude. Reducing uncertainty means that the task must take on meaning for members of the team. If you want to lead, you must capture the meaning of each task and transmit it to your team or find out if someone has already identified it and get the group to listen to that person. You cannot do any of these things without both perspectives or without being able to combine them correctly. For the latter, you will need to prepare yourself mentally to overcome all the prejudices and conventions that distort and limit your vision. Once again, if you want others to change, you have to change yourself first.

To create an open vision, Peter Senge's *The Fifth Discipline* (1990), a true bible of systemic thought, lays out what he calls the laws of the Fifth Discipline.

1. **Today's problems come from yesterday's solution.** You cannot transfer your problems to another part of the system hoping that they will be resolved. Passing the buck won't cut it.

2. **The harder you push, the harder the system pushes back.** When our initial efforts don't yield lasting improvements, we press harder, believing that this will help us overcome the obstacles, without realizing that we are creating bigger ones. For example, when someone quits smoking he gains weight, his self-esteem drops, and he wants to smoke to relieve the stress. Willpower alone isn't enough. You have to understand how the system works in order to change it.

3. **Behavior gets better before it gets worse.** Feedback usually involves a delay or lag between the short-term benefit and the long-term damage. A solution that you think will cure the symptoms may bring the problem back later or create a bigger one. I remember a personal experience in a pharmaceutical company in which management drastically reduced the sales team's lunch budget to cut costs. At first, the drop in spending was spectacular. As time went on, though, salespeople were setting up more client meetings so that they could eat with doctors every day and as a result, the company's client entertainment expenses went through the roof!

4. **The easy way out usually leads back in.** We are all comfortable applying proven solutions to problems. Insistence on these known

solutions—while fundamental problems persist or get worse—is a good indicator of localized thinking. This is the "We need a bigger hammer" syndrome, but what if you need a screwdriver?

5. **The cure can be worse than the disease.** The most insidious consequence of applying localized solutions is that each instance requires more of the same. For example, you build a beltway in a city to reduce congestion. The new road encourages vehicle use in a major metropolitan area, increases traffic, and, as a result, increases congestion. Any long-term solution should reinforce the system's ability to cope with its own burdens.

6. **Faster is slower.** It's the tale of the tortoise and the hare. Slow and steady wins the race! Systemic thinking is more challenging than our usual way of tackling problems, so it can take more time to come to a solution.

7. **Cause and effect are not closely related in time and space.** We tend to think of cause and effect as always being closely related. However, that's a mere delusion of our thinking that has developed after many years of simple approaches. We are now discovering complexity and see that often this is not the case.

8. **Small changes can produce big results—but the areas of highest leverage are often the least obvious.** Facing a difficult problem requires finding the leverage point—the change that with minimal effort leads to significant improvement. There are no simple rules to effecting high leverage changes, but there are ways of thinking that can help. You must learn to see underlying structures in the system instead of specific events. You must also think in terms of processes and not in static clichés.

9. **You can have your cake and eat it too—but not all at once.** Sometimes, the most complicated problems can be simple when viewed from a systemic perspective. They are a product of snapshot thinking, not process thinking, and can be viewed in a new light if we consider their evolution over time.

10. **Dividing an elephant in half does not produce two small elephants.** The analytical mentality that we have traditionally cultivated shows us how to pick apart a problem to resolve individual pieces. However, this doesn't always work the way we had hoped because to understand the majority of managerial problems you must understand the complex nature of the system that generates them. The same thing happens in reverse. Grouping elements isn't good enough. There is an old saying in the United States that sums it up nicely: "Two turkeys don't make an eagle."

11. **There is no blame.** We tend to blame our problems on external circumstances. Being the object of criticism to reduce tension ends up being one of the main functions of a company's leadership or a country's government. Systemic thinking shows that nothing is external; we and the source of our problems are a part of the same system. The solution, again, is managing our relationship with our adversary.

12. **See the wood for the trees.** The art of systemic thinking is being able to recognize subtle structures of increasing complexity and dynamics. In fact, the essence of mastering systemic thinking lies in seeing patterns where others only see events.

To summarize, how does Peter Senge view the systemic role of the leader? Let's review how he outlines it in *The Fifth Discipline* (1990), "In a learning organization, leaders are designers, stewards, and teachers. They are responsible for building organizations where people continually expand their capabilities to understand complexity, clarify vision, and improve shared mental models—that is, they are responsible for learning."

What Challenges Does a Leader Face on a Systemic Level?

Continuing with Senge, let's take a look at what he outlines as the seven learning disabilities that a leader should be able to overcome in order to help others do the same:

1. **I am my position.** We envelop ourselves in our functions and tasks, not in the company's purpose. We end up believing that we are what we do and can get carried away with it. We feel responsible for it and are barely aware of the consequences that our actions have on the rest of the organization.

   But when we cultivate a systemic view, we make ourselves aware of these interrelations and evolve from responsibility to co-responsibility. We move from merely being responsible for our tasks to adopting shared responsibility with others over the outcomes of the organization.

2. **The enemy is out there.** When humans face poor results, our first response is to justify ourselves and transfer blame to other people or outside agents. Only when this is not possible do we proceed to review our plans and actions.

   It's easy for organizations to incorporate this tendency into the corporate culture. The marketing department blames production, "We keep losing sales because our quality is not competitive." Production blames engineering, "The designs are inefficient." And engineering blames marketing, "They load us full of complications." The cycle continues on from there.

   The idea of an external adversary is actually a byproduct of the belief that "I am my position." When we focus only on our work, we do not see how our own actions extend beyond their boundary. When those actions have consequences that come back to hurt us, we misinterpret these new problems as having an external origin.

3. **The illusion of taking charge.** A proactive attitude is often viewed as an antidote against being reactive, or waiting until a situation is out of control before doing something about it. When a manager is being proactive or assertive—when she rolls up her sleeves—she often feels emotionally gratified and justified: She's working, sometimes fiercely, for the good of the organization, but is that really the case? Is she doing it from her particular vision or from her particular interest? How often is proactivity nothing more than reactivity

in disguise? ("We are going to fix the mess that the factory put us in.") True proactivity comes from seeing how we can improve the system.

4. **The fixation on events.** We are conditioned to see life as a series of events and to believe that for every event there is one cause. Obsessing over events and data dominates our meetings: last month's sales, the new budget cuts, last quarter's earnings, who just got promoted or fired, our competitor's new product, a delay in a new product launch, or similar.

As Senge explains, "The media reinforces an emphasis on short-term events—after all, if it's more than two days' old it's no longer 'news.' Focusing on events leads to 'event' explanations: 'The Dow Jones average dropped sixteen points today,' announces the newspaper, 'because low fourth-quarter profits were announced yesterday.' Such explanations may be true as far as they go, but they distract us from seeing the longer-term patterns of change that lie behind the events and from understanding the causes of those patterns." Today, the biggest threats to our survival, from our organizations to our societies, come not from sudden events, but from slow and gradual processes: the arms race, environmental decay, the erosion of the educational system, gradual losses in competitiveness, and so on.

For that reason, an organizational learning culture must understand processes. If we focus on events, at most we can predict an event before it happens and react accordingly. But if we only have that one perception, we cannot learn to create. This conditioning is very common in our business culture. Other cultures have broader visions that, over time, can become genuine competitive advantages for them. I am reminded of an anecdote from a trip I took to China. We were going through a new commercial area in Shanghai composed of no fewer than 40 recently completed skyscrapers. This was one of many areas in the city that had recently sprung up in just five years. I asked our Chinese companion if the properties were occupied and he said no. I replied that I did not see how such an investment could be profitable. He merely replied with a phrase that will always stick with me: "you have to build nests if you want the birds to come." They will come. Guaranteed.

5. **The parable of the boiled frog.** Poor adaptation to gradually building threats to survival is so pervasive in systems studies of corporate failure that it has given rise to the parable of the boiled frog. If you place a frog in a pot of boiling water, it will immediately try to escape. But if you place the frog in room temperature water, and don't scare him, he'll stay calm and allow you to gradually heat the water. The frog will become groggier and groggier, until he is unable to climb out and is boiled. To survive, evolution has made the frog aware of sudden changes to its environment, but it is not prepared to face slow and gradual threats. We often behave like the frog, watching for sudden movements. To detect slow and gradual processes you need a different perspective and a different pace of response. And that is how we often get cooked.

6. **The delusion of learning from experience.** "We each have a learning horizon, a breadth of vision in time and space, within which we assess our effectiveness," Senge explains. "When our actions have consequences beyond our learning horizon, it becomes impossible to learn from direct experience." This is a key point for organizations: We learn from experience, but what happens when we do not directly experience the consequences of many of our decisions? An organization's most important decisions have consequences throughout the entire system, often beyond what we can even see. And they can have an effect for years.

Large organizations combat complexity by dividing themselves into components: They create flowcharts and hierarchies to bring decisions closer to the problem. The price they pay is the loss of a cohesive vision: Functional divisions transform into fiefdoms, analysis of complex problems that go beyond functional lines suffers, and the organization gets further away from a systemic vision. When those mental compartments are incorporated into the organization's culture, they are hard to eliminate. I remember the case of a publishing company that tried to do it by replacing its management group's key positions with people from outside the organization. In less than a year they had already become "feudal lords"! With a much more modern style, of course.

7. **The myth of the management team.** Often, business teams will spend time fighting to defend their territory, avoiding anything that might make them personally look bad. Since being in conflict is usually frowned upon, members of the team will try to portray an image of cohesion, hiding their disputes, silencing anything they think could negatively affect them, and saying only what is expected of them. Instead of evolving through management that is healthy and constructive in the face of conflict, the conflict gets buried. Obviously, this brings down the level of debate and hurts the capacity for vision. But, overall, it reduces individual commitment with respect to the decisions and agreements adopted by the group.

Making the organization aware of these traps in favor of growth and learning means that a leader must first keep himself alert and aware. Secondly, it means being able to spread this systemic awareness by example and creating opportunities and forums for debate and reflection (Senge 1990).

Vulnerability, Acceptance, Learning, and Growth

As Chris Argyris, professor emeritus at Harvard Business School, is quoted in *The Fifth Discipline* (1990): "Most management teams break down under pressure. The team may function quite well with routine issues. But when they confront complex issues that may be embarrassing or threatening, the *teamness* seems to go to pot."

The bonds of a team rest on a foundation of trust. And a team only has real trust when its members are able to show their vulnerability in front of the rest without fear of it being used against them. That trust makes honest communication possible. It is the basis of good debate where everyone speaks and everyone is heard, in which decisions are accepted by all. That is how you create genuine commitment.

However, our social education does not help us recognize what we don't know—or are afraid of—and the majority of companies reinforce this idea by not rewarding people who risk plunging themselves into complex problems. When was the last time that someone in your organization was rewarded for questioning a company policy instead of resolving an urgent problem?

In the face of uncertainty or ignorance, we learn to ignore problems and move on. "No problem. Keep working." This process blocks our understanding of the threat, as well as our own reaction to it. Conversely, if we do not accept that we are facing something that we don't know or understand, we cannot open ourselves up to learning.

In conclusion, cultivating a systemic vision requires planting and cultivating an apprentice's spirit, one that's open to learning and unlearning. In a systemic view, what's intuitive is often not what's best and what's best is often not intuitive. We have to constantly challenge these traditional associations of cause and effect that we find so attractive. Being aware that you are part of a system means knowing that cooperation is more useful than internal competition and that thinking of others matters most.

A systemic vision of leadership brings us closer to what we earlier considered its essence: helping the team maintain a constructive focus in the face of a threat or change. And ensuring focus through learning and personal and professional growth, which first demands accepting vulnerability.

5

Leader and Boss

Let's now take a look at some of my own first-hand experiences from a few years back. They remind me just how true that expression "life imitates art" really is.

Real Experience Number 1

The month was coming to an end. The boss was talking to me in the hall about the state of sales. We were all living through a widespread economic crisis, the situation was tough, and no news about the situation was ever good. He felt insecure and needed to display his power and dominance. He pivoted skillfully and delivered an agile kick to the divider of the adjacent office. He was a karate master. The boss could do these sorts of things!

The divider resisted, but fell over. After a few confused seconds, the office door opened and in popped my surprised neighbor, a division director. After a brief stare that was both ironic and defiant, the boss blurted out: "What? Did I wake you?" He then left the room, pleased with himself. Where would this company be without that man?

Real Experience Number 2

A new project took me to the headquarters of the multinational corporation I worked for. I had a pre-launch meeting with members of the purchasing department. We had never met and I had hardly ever spoken to any of them on the phone.

It was a cold and foggy day, which is typical of northern Italy, where the company started more than 50 years ago. However, the welcome I received was very warm, which comforted me. Here were two members of the old guard, real veterans in the company, receiving a young marketing professional who presumably came to make their lives difficult.

A few minutes into the meeting, one of them smiled at me serenely and asked, out of nowhere, about my boss: "How are things going for Mr. B. in Spain?" Unsure of his intentions, I replied, biding my time: "Good, good. Why do you ask?"

The other gentleman was more direct and answered me snidely: "We're just curious. After everything we went through to send him over there! We all had to agree to recommend him as the ideal manager for Spain." In his eyes, I saw a sense of pride.

Real Experience Number 3

We were meeting in the boss's office. There were five of us, all marketing and sales executives except for the boss, revising the business strategy for the next quarter. The meeting went along normally. Suddenly, something irritated the boss. He jumped to his feet, went through a series of stretches, accompanied by loud breathing noises, and proceeded to punch and kick his chair, which was thankfully vacant. Then, having calmed down, he sat back down and continued the debate.

But that's not the real anecdote. The curious thing is that throughout this entire episode, the rest of us just kept working unperturbed, as if nothing were happening! And again, it was a spontaneous act.

Management and Leadership

I promise that those were real events. Writing them now, they seem more humorous than dramatic. That's why I chose them; they're illustrative in that endearingly humorous sense that permeates memories. Yes, our brains can be quite generous with our memories! It softens them up and keeps only the best parts. But in that moment, they were anything but funny. They were more like a strong source of uncertainty and stress. I felt like I was dragged far away from professional achievement.

I speak from experience. At one time in my career, I was at the beck and call of someone who today would be categorized as an organizational psychopath, a shady character who doled out unhappiness. He was tremendously gifted in his work, which made him all the more damaging to the organization. All of his superiors knew he was difficult, but they couldn't care less because he produced results, in the short-term, anyway.

Without reaching pathological extremes, some command and control management styles can negatively affect the performance of teams. They can even form—or deform—an organization's corporate culture, giving rise to what is called an authoritarian management style.

At this point, we should link back to the anecdotes with which we opened this chapter. I selected them because they clearly show two key points:

- How important managing one's own ego is for executive conduct.
- Teams defend themselves from bosses.

And now we can start to delve deeper. Away we go!

Management Style and Ego

The true value of a human being is determined primarily by the measure and sense in which he has attained to liberation from the self.

—Albert Einstein, *The World As I See It*

Fear. Within it lives the primary difference between the emotional impact of the boss and the leader. The former increases fear and the latter reduces it.

Ego is the software we need to survive as individuals. It is what makes you feel like you, a unique person who is different from the rest, who wants to live, and has the right to do so. The ego is the piece of individual mental survival software that allows the caveman inside you to claim its meat when it is divvied up around the fire.

> The ego's function is not to make you fairer, wiser, or happier. It is only to ensure that you survive. If someone has to fall, let it be someone else.

When you as a manager are faced with an atmosphere of uncertainty, insecurities will flare up. They provoke feelings of anxiety and fear, which are designed to put you in a state of alertness to keep you on guard against what you perceive as a threat. Your ego immediately jumps into action to come to your aid and take over. Therefore, when you are afraid (if you haven't yet mastered self-management) your ego will naturally take charge of your work and your life. And your ego will do what it knows how to do, that which gives meaning to its existence: survival at all costs.

How? You know from experience. Your ego will take steps to protect itself and take control of the situation. It will not hesitate to use all the resources that the organization has put at your disposal, which is to say, power. At this point, you might not be aware of it, but you'll be quickly on your way to acting like a boss. That may not be your intention, but I'm afraid it's not up to you—the context has provoked the situation.

When you are made responsible for a department or team, you take on a role in the system that will force you, from the very beginning, to confront two important factors:

- Those below you didn't elect you. I'm sure you deserve that promotion, but nobody on your team voted for you. If anything, someone above you did. You were elected by a superior power.

- The position you will take requires managing a certain level of power that's intrinsic to that position in the organization.

Notice that, like it or not, just receiving the promotion means that you are a boss. Whether or not you will be a leader remains to be seen, but you cannot escape being a boss. Make no mistake, that fact changes things. You probably have already noticed changes in your behavior and outlook on the job. In the worst case, you may experience a flaring up of latent psychopathic behavior. It's clear that power affects us, so we must strive to ensure that our behavior doesn't run wild and that we stay connected to our genuine selves.

One extreme example of how power can affect us comes from a famous Soviet autocrat, Joseph Stalin, who in 1923 explained his greatest pleasure in life to two comrades: "The greatest pleasure is to choose one's enemies, prepare one's plans minutely, slake an implacable vengeance, and then go to bed" (Service 2004). There's nothing like a job well done to make you feel good and sleep like a baby.

The Boss

As we have just seen, the boss figure rests on the use of power. The word *power* comes from the Latin *potestas*. In Roman law, this term defines the legal right to enforce a decision, which implies having the strength to do so, that is, the ability to punish. It is worlds apart from *authority* (*auctoritas*), socially recognized wisdom, which is held by those who have influence by virtue of their judgment and personality. Therefore, with power inevitably comes the capacity for control and repression. As a result, where there is power, there is fear. Fear of punishment for the controlled and fear of losing power for the boss.

Power gives the boss, or the boss's ego, a level of security, recognition, and prestige in the organization. And the famous erotic poetry of power is born—our beloved boss's ego is fed, gets plump and beautiful, and always wants more. If this process is not balanced by a personal self-awareness effort or some healthy failure that keeps his feet on the ground, it's easy to lose control. Without that balance, the ego starts working against its host and ultimately enslaves it.

If you are or have been a manager, you know what I mean: The moment you find yourself fighting to have the flashiest car, the best office, or even a mere plant, look out! It's an endless process that could drag any professional into a deep internal void and a permanent sense of insecurity. It gets worse with age, continued changes, and the arrival of young and hungry generations who are full of ego and energy.

> Once you develop an affinity for power and an awareness that you could lose it, fear begets more fear and your priorities change. You will use your power to maintain it and not to build or create.

On the other hand, the pact made with those below is also perverse. They sell their souls to the devil (the boss) and accept fear in exchange for two advantages, unloading onto the boss two heavy burdens:

- the weight of uncertainty, gaining a certain sense of security—"it's not my job to worry about that"
- the weight of responsibility—"I just follow orders."

In a way, you end up with a sort of infantilization, a loss of the maturity of being responsible for your own life and your decisions. The first victim in this is the truth. You avoid everything that could jeopardize that fragile status quo. The second victim is commitment. Your team's performance will inevitably suffer. Consequently the organization that's based on power can provide some sense of security and order, but is ultimately inefficient.

Bear in mind that many people would be willing to make a pact like this one! Just look at what happens when one of those long-term dictators dies—history is full of recent examples. Pay attention to the faces of those following the coffin: More than sadness, the faces of the deceased's supporters show helplessness! Go ahead and see for yourself. Find a good nonverbal communication handbook and look for images of your favorite autocrat's funeral online. Just note that it's more noticeable on film than in photos.

In summary, we can infer that the use of power is based on a game of personal insecurities, which in the extreme leads to a mutual dependence between boss and subordinates. In this game, fear becomes the true relational currency that's exchanged between members of the group: Either the circumstances, the boss, or a combination of both put fear on the market and the players pass it around, getting more exhausted each time, but they're unable to quit the game.

The time will come when they can't conceive of other possibilities or think of the world being different. That is the real harm of autocratic systems. Self-censorship rules the land. The players' brains only work on the defensive. They are pumped full of cortisol (stress) and they stop thinking, creating, and imagining. How many people walk into work in the morning and hang up not only their coat but also their life? They cease to be creative and entrepreneurial. All of this inevitably makes the group lose its competitive edge. This process is reached in several ways, broken down into two major currents that we will call "failure highways":

- The blocking highway, which creates fear in our brain, makes us incapable of seeing opportunities and fighting uncertainty through innovation and creativity. Fear muddies our brain and causes us to lose the ability to adapt.

- The Machiavellian highway drags us swiftly toward a sort of perverse order of priorities. The end result is less important than conserving power in those above and maintaining the status of those below. Or, as we have all heard at some point, "no one at this company cares about the client." That is, until the competition wipes them out.

However, the boss is necessary. It's a role of the system, one that wields power, but only when the circumstances demand timely and decisive action and don't allow for debate, doubt, or hesitation. That is to say, management of what should be the exceptions.

In fact, the majority of emergencies that a team encounters (not including natural catastrophes) are a result of the group not doing their homework or heeding the warnings. They're a failure of vision or an excess of ego. These failures are an example of systemic selfishness. People weren't paying attention to what was important. They were only focusing on what seemed important from the perspective of the mental box they had been living in.

History shows that facts are very cruel to our mental boxes. How can you avoid such a perverse dynamic? Well, for that there is another system role that makes this its critical mission: the leader.

The Leader

As we saw already, Roman law understood authority as the moral capacity to give an opinion and be taken seriously during a decision. That opinion is not legally binding and cannot be imposed, but it does hold a very strong value. Today we'd say that a person with authority has good judgment and influence.

The word *authority* does not cease to be a degenerative form of the original meaning simply because it has been hijacked over time by bosses to mean exactly the opposite: for example, we talk of "an authoritarian political regime" when referring to a dictatorship. The original meaning has only persevered in the fields that are the most distant from power, such as the scientific and cultural. There we still say "that person is an authority on the subject." Notice, also, the enormous difference in meaning between the expressions *to have influence* (pure authority) and *to have connections* (which alludes to the power of having close ties to powerful people).

> The boss and the leader are from two worlds that occupy the same space, but are completely different from one another: the world of getting people to do and the world of getting people to want to do.

The boss manages by force, the power to impose and enforce policies, so that people carry out certain behaviors and repress others. In sum, power is the capacity to punish and reward. And the person who wields that power will do so as long as he has the capacity, regardless of how he came to have it. In other words, whether acquired by means of a democratic election or a promotion handed down from someone more powerful, the person in power manages both the carrot and the stick. It's completely unimportant if the people who depend on him believe in his decision. They will have to adhere to it, like it or not. And the tool used for this is called commanding or giving orders. To command effectively you just need to give clear and concrete instructions about:

- the behavior expected of the group
- how that behavior will be evaluated
- the consequences of adhering to or defying those expectations.

These days you don't even need to have a loud voice, although it doesn't hurt! The implicit meaning of commanding is to demand certain actions or behaviors of people, regardless of their perspective or feelings. The process of commanding doesn't require the boss to be concerned with whether or not the team likes the orders or how they are affected by them. Of course, this doesn't mean that those things don't have repercussions down the line. The expression *extrinsic motivation* (motivation from outside the individual) is often used to discuss this type of reward and punishment as essential parts of the boss's role.

In contrast, the meaning of *leading* is completely different: fostering the impulse or desire in people to effect specific actions or behaviors as a result of their perspective and feelings. The leader builds from within, from people's intrinsic motivation (their internal engine). To do so requires hitting certain keys, including some very deep ones, which we will develop in later chapters.

At the end of this chapter you will find a diagram explaining the sequence of human behavior from its inception, clearly differentiating the scope of management's two territories: the leader and the boss. The diagram will also indicate where each management tool comes into play, as discussed in Part III.

Boss and Leader

As we've seen, when you are given the responsibility to take charge of a department, you are given power. Leadership, on the other hand, must be won. The relational nature of leadership lays out its own rules: Only the team can decide if it will establish a leadership relationship with you. In the same way that we cannot force anyone to be our friend, we cannot force a leadership relationship. So it goes.

They may have given you power and you may demand that others obey you, but getting people to follow you willingly is another matter. That must be won. That decision is the team's prerogative. So they can tell you to "manage this team," but if they say "we're naming you leader of this project," take it with a grain of salt. Be grateful and get ready to fight for your leadership or, if you fail, to at least be a good boss. That's not easy either.

If you achieve leadership, you will have to nurture it so that it develops for the good of the group. And here you will find one of the most classic (and little-known) management problems: How you balance being a boss and a leader will define your management style. But how do you combine two roles—boss and leader—that require often contradictory behaviors? You will find yourself in two simultaneous and permanently counteracting tensions:

- Despite how much leadership you have achieved, there will always be situations where you have to pound your fist on the table. Anyone who has managed groups knows it, even if the leadership handbooks are reluctant to admit it.

- On the other hand, commanding usually reduces the team's efficiency: People may roll up their sleeves, but detach their hearts and minds from the task at hand. Abusing your power means definitively killing your chances for leadership and negatively impacting results.

Let's not kid ourselves here. Managing these forces requires perpetually fine-tuning a dynamic equilibrium. It requires the craftsmanship of developing tailor-made solutions to every problem to safeguard a method that gives coherence and promise to our actions. As a reference for the road ahead, I'll offer a metaphor that may be helpful in your reflections. Imagine that you've opened an account at the World Bank of Leadership, an institution created specifically to develop humanity's riches through leadership development. Upon opening the account, you're informed that each time you act as a leader, your balance will grow proportionate with the quality of your behavior. In contrast, every time you act like a boss, your account will shrink, also in proportion to the scale of your blunder.

As long as your ledger is in the black, you will predominantly be a leader. Pounding your fist on the table will bring your team to think "He has his reasons. . . ." However, when your ledger is in the red, watch out! You are entering dictatorial territory.

How can I check my balance?

Well, that's the interesting part! There is only one way to know for sure: Your team will tell you. How? Learn to continually read their nonverbal communication. Leadership is something that is felt more than anything. What if you don't achieve leadership in your team? In that case, don't fret or lose sleep over it. Focus your energy on being a good boss. Leadership is a role of the team and what's important is that it exists and that the team has a leader, even if it's not you.

When the boss doesn't also achieve leadership, some titleless leader will inexorably emerge, who we call the informal leader. If you can work with that person, the team will function just fine because both roles will be present. Surely, you've seen some war movie in which the novice lieutenant cooperates with the veteran sergeant and things just work out. For it to go well, you need to be able to do the following:

- Accept that you aren't achieving leadership of your team.

- Accept the emergence of an informal leader.

- Be sufficiently secure in yourself to resist seeing that informal leader as a threat.

- Be impartial enough to determine if that informal leader can sufficiently contribute to the team's success while avoiding self-deception.

- Establish an alliance with the informal leader.

If you achieve this, my hat's off to you. You are a good boss! Sure, being a leader is more fashionable these days, but if companies were filled with good bosses, leadership could flow freely. And experience has taught me that being a good boss often results in genuine leadership training. In contrast, if you are an insecure or reactive person who views informal leadership as a threat, you'll find a way to get rid of anyone who takes on that role until your team is a wasteland. If this sounds like you, go out and find yourself a good coach fast. Hire the best one you can find. You will thank me!

Not willing to put in the work? Then with all of your energy make decisions, act, give out instructions, and get out while you can! Before your results catch up with you.

Red Flags

The following is a collection of very common phrases that will help you detect danger. When you catch yourself saying one of them, or if you hear them from your direct reports, look out! The leadership in your team is at risk:

- If I didn't do everything around here. . .
- The moment I turn away. . .
- They're just stupid.
- These people aren't motivated.
- My people don't want to work.
- I saw that coming.
- I've warned her about this.
- I wish I could trust them, but I can't.
- This place is the Wild West.

FIGURE 5.1: THE LEADER'S TERRITORY (WANTING TO DO)

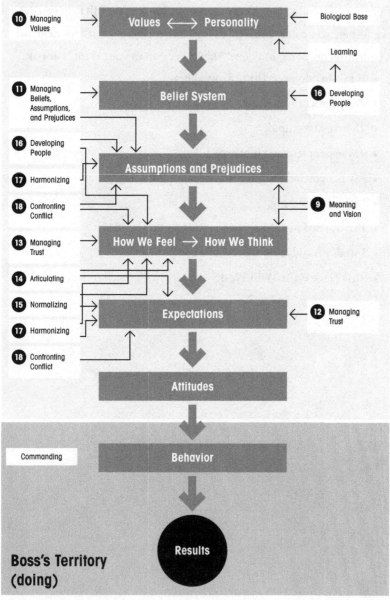

NOTE: The numbers correspond to chapters.

PART II

Ideas That Do Not Help

6

Idea Number 1: I Am a Leader

After decades of searching for the defining characteristics of a leader, science seems to have come to the conclusion that it's a useless effort. Basically, it's because leadership isn't a quality of a leader, but rather a systemic and relational role.

Let's remember that leadership is a type of human relationship that is established between one member of the group and the rest. The group trusts the leader to guide them in what she feels is the best path for everyone. As a relationship, leadership is similar to other types of relationships, for example, friendship, love, coaching, or even that between a client and vendor.

Which friend owns a friendship between two people? Who is responsible for it? It obviously belongs to both of them. They share it, contribute to it, and nurture it. In fact, even if it were not a symmetrical relationship, it would require acceptance and commitment on both sides. All of this is assumed naturally and neither would think to say with a straight face, "I am the friend here." If anything, we would say, "I am your friend" or "we are friends."

However, it's not uncommon to hear "Antonio is a leader" or "I am the leader of this project." People also talk about born leaders. Thinking of leadership as a characteristic or quality to be possessed is risky for someone in a leadership role. Let's see why.

High-quality leadership requires two essential values: humility and generosity. Humility is necessary to keep the leader from losing sight of the fact that it was the group that gave her this role and that the group can take it away. Generosity ensures that the leader works for the common good and not for herself. Remember that the difference between a leader and a manipulator isn't in the techniques they use, which are practically the same. The differences are in intent and awareness.

When a leader treats leadership like a quality he possesses, he unknowingly starts a journey toward decadence. He slowly stops thinking of the group and starts thinking for the group instead. This erodes his connection with his people. Listening and convincing become uncomfortable and thankless tasks, especially the latter. It starts to show in the way he expresses himself: "after everything I've done for them, this is how they repay me." And the ego echoes: "if it weren't for me." He inches closer to the dangerous abyss of self-centeredness and often drags the team down with him: "It's my team. It's mine or it's nobody's."

The leader is there to serve the group and must never lose sight of that. When a leader gets carried away with her ego, she starts to make decisions for the group ("I know what they want" or "I know what's best for them"). She gradually trades critical collaborators (who can be uncomfortable but enriching members of the team) for those who tell her what she wants to hear. Communication with the group, trust, and decision-making will suffer. Individual commitment will deteriorate and it will become "every man for himself." This is a process known as going off the rails. The same things that have helped us grow can sink us, diminishing our self awareness and ability for adaptation. No person who undertakes leadership for long enough is immune to this virus. Avoiding it requires a constant and willing effort by the leader.

Thinking of leadership as a personal quality can also invite a lesser danger, that of dependence. During a long enough period of time, we get used to being the focal point and being important to the organization. At that moment, we start to feel and fear the risk of losing that status. Consequently, our role will cease to be ours and we will gradually become possessed by it. We will start to make self-serving decisions, opting for "popular" choices—those choices that others want to hear, not the ones that force us to convince them of things at the risk of them being rejected.

Notice that you cannot own leadership, but you can certainly feel like you do! When we feel like we own leadership, the idea that we only possess what we are willing to let go of becomes our biggest risk, because what we aren't willing to let go of, in reality, possesses us. And living leadership like a quality that we possess is no exception.

7

Idea Number 2: Objectivity

I am subjective because I am a subject. If I were
objective, I would be an object.

—Miguel de Unamuno

Man is the measure of all things: of the things which are, that they
are, and of things which are not, that they are not.

—Protagoras

For centuries, Western thinkers have been developing an almost cult-like
following of reason and logic and, as a result, its natural offspring: objectivity. This focus, which devours all other paths of knowledge, has started to
become relativized since the dawn of the neurosciences and the concept of
emotional intelligence. We now know that humans are specifically designed
to not be objective.

In fact, there are few activities in which we actually can act objectively,
for example, those in which we are not emotionally involved in at all, like
mathematical computation. In any given situation, our emotional response
is thousands of times faster than our rational thought. As Antonio Damasio
put it in his book *Descartes' Error* (1994), first we feel, then we think. And our
thoughts will change depending on those feelings!

To sum it up simply and explicitly, our brain shows two types of behavior: one that is proactive and creative and another that is reactive and defensive. The key to which type gets triggered depends on which of our emotions prevail. This process takes place in the area of the brain known as the limbic system. So when we experience a situation coming from a place of hope, we have access to more power from the areas of the brain that deal with creativity, learning, the meaning of life, and so on. And we reduce activity in areas that deal with fear. As a result, we feel more capable and motivated. In contrast, if our insecurities are heightened, then the process develops in the opposite direction. Our fears flare up and creativity and learning become inhibited.

> We are incapable of separating emotion and thought in the vast majority of our activities. Remembering back to Antonio Damasio, man is not a rational being. Man is a being that rationalizes over an emotional base that ultimately conditions its thoughts.

Given this knowledge, don't get bogged down seeking out objectivity. You will not find it. You will, however, find that awareness of your emotions is very useful. It will offer you a wealth of valuable information with which to govern your life. Remember, from an early age we are taught how to control emotions, not manage them, and the difference is huge:

- By controlling emotions, we seek to put a lid on them and act as if they don't exist.

- Conversely, managing emotions means listening to them, accepting them, and then learning how to make decisions with those emotions in mind. This will lead to resonant decisions that commit us more and mobilize our energy better, which will be noticeable in the results.

If you accept and engage the task of managing your emotions, you will open up the door for those around you to do the same. And that, too, is leadership.

8

Idea Number 3: Flexibility

One option makes you a robot. Two options create a dilemma.
More than two and you are truly free.

—John Grinder

"I've seen other crises in the past, but I have a feeling that this time is different."

John is worried. He's 40 and has a comfortable life, as he will tell you. He considers himself a well-centered person with a solid and stable family and career. He's always done what's right. He feels like he fits in and is valued by those around him.

Recently, he's noticed some disturbing and dramatic changes. His friends, good, hard-working people, are finding themselves unemployed, just like that. Work is pressuring him to learn new procedures and suggesting he take more professional development training. "College used to be enough." His neighborhood is changing every day. Friends are getting divorced. "Who would have guessed it?" Things that happen in China have a direct impact at home. He believes that society has become a place where "anything goes. People have no principles anymore. Nobody prepared me for this."

John considers himself a flexible guy, but he gets the feeling that lately he's coming up short. He can't shake this nagging feeling of uncertainty, which leads to insecurity. He has a sense that he doesn't know what's going on and, most importantly, he doesn't know what to do about it. He's stressed and not sleeping well.

His son, Zander (the name John seemed so unoriginal at the time, and they had just seen this movie . . . You know the story. It turns out that now the name John is more original than ever!) is 12 years old. Even at his age, he already acts like a teen. He plays with gadgets that John barely understands and he finds his father's childhood games boring. He loves new technology and takes to it like a fish to water. But he quickly gets bored with things and lacks perseverance. And he talks to friends on social networks more than he does in person.

If he's lucky, Zander will live well beyond the age of 90 and will probably change careers (not jobs) at least four times. Today we can't even begin to imagine some of those careers. His life will be so different from his father's!

In some way, they both sense that what will differentiate their lives will depend on their thought processes, their value systems, and the beliefs that support them. Accelerated technological change has put John into an experimental generation. He is living through things that have never happened before and for which his upbringing hasn't prepared him. Quite the opposite: He will have to unlearn if he wants to move forward!

In contrast, Zander absorbs everything easily and it fascinates him. Even John's inherited belief system is primarily aimed at combating uncertainty and seeking out stability. It gives more weight to the dangers of change than the opportunities it implies. In the end, "better the devil you know than the devil you don't," right? But Zander's thought structure is being built to coexist with uncertainty and make the most out of it.

Let's look at John's cultural inheritance. If, for example, we look at definitions for terms such as *flexible, fold,* or *adapt* in Merriam-Webster's dictionary, we get significant clues. The definitions transmit a reactive attitude in the face of an undesirable and unavoidable situation, something that happens to us and is lived more with resignation than acceptance: to change without wanting to be changed.

But why is it so hard for John to approach it like Zander would? Basically, changes often require us to modify our mental schemes, but we identify with them and with our belief systems so much that we think we simply are our beliefs. And this fact complicates change. Note: Change depends less on our age and more on how prepared we are for it! If we learn how to modify our beliefs and practice changing, this ability to change will stick with us our whole lives.

A friend of mine, a graphic designer, once told me that "there are designers who only create what their software will allow, software that is powerful, but limiting to their creativity." He added, "Who's in charge? The software or them?"

So what kinds of designers of our own lives do we want to be? Our beliefs are the mental software that we use to structure our lives, but they are not our lives! It's important for us to learn to modify the software so that we're in charge.

Neuroscience has shown that our capacity for change is very high, but it fails to stimulate certain creative and learning-based brain circuits situated in the left prefrontal cortex. These circuits are only activated when we experience a situation optimistically. In contrast, living in fear or pain stimulates other more defensive brain circuits that close us off and start a chain of stress processes.

When we know we should accept change, but we resist it emotionally, the result is not true acceptance. That has another name: resignation. When we are able to decide how we want to experience a certain situation, our ability to find new methods multiplies and change becomes possible, even tempting! Wanting to decide how to experience a situation also has a name: proactivity.

Thus, being flexible today is not simply accepting. It means being willing to go beyond that and actually wanting to change. But this mental process is not innate because it requires learning and training. Our education limits us: Nobody ever told John that he also works like this or even explained how to be efficient in and learn from change. Like John, we have been taught to control ourselves, not to manage ourselves. That's where emotional repression and stress come from.

Ultimately, what we call adaptation is often, in fact, resignation. And where there is resignation there is no proactivity. Only resistance and, frequently, despair.

With the advancement of neuroscience and neuro-linguistic programming (NLP), we get new and effective techniques for moving from controlling emotions to managing them. We move from understanding how we are living a situation to deciding how we want to live it. Such techniques will one day, no doubt, be taught in school!

In conclusion, changes in the real world require increased flexibility, but from a new paradigm based on living situations from a place of proactivity and not from resignation. We should, from now on, define flexibility in a new way—as the resulting competency of a combination of abilities:

- being aware of how we live in a certain situation
- knowing how to manage our emotions (especially fear) to maintain a clear and open mind
- learning to create new perspectives that inspire and motivate us.

That way we can discover and create opportunities and generate the necessary energy to convert them into action.

Today we start knowing what to do and how to do it. The solution is right at our fingertips. All that's left is to get into gear!

PART III

Leadership Tools

9

Meaning and Vision

Millions long for immortality who don't know what to do
with themselves on a rainy Sunday afternoon.

—Susan Ertz, *Anger in the Sky*

If a man hasn't discovered something that he will
die for, he isn't fit to live.

—Martin Luther King Jr., Detroit, June 23, 1963

We are all interested in the future, for that is where you
and I are going to spend the rest of our lives.

—Woody Allen, *Plan 9 From Outer Space*

A Preliminary Explanation
for Workaholics

Beware the traps that we set for ourselves! In this chapter, we will discuss
meaning and vision. Living your job intensely and making it part of your
life's essence will really allow you to enjoy it and maximize your efficiency.
Feeling work this way could even bring you to see it as a mission. However,
that does not necessarily imply that the work is your life. Many people think
that they are what they do, but that's not true: The belief that we are much

more than our job is something that we have to uncover over time and is also necessary to live.

> If you are only what you do, you cease to be the moment you stop doing it.

If you are only what you do, what is left when you stop? The answer is often "nothing" or "I don't know." But we only figure it out when the circumstances force us to stop. This is very common in people who retire or are laid off, if they haven't tried to understand who they are beyond the job or, better yet, who they could be. In our civilization, we aren't taught to figure this out and, without knowing it, we can go our whole lives simply going to and from work.

If we can't enrich our lives to find meaning in other facets that balance us out or fill our lives with activities that help us grow, we will end up languishing in an internal void or slipping into hopeless depression. We need to regenerate and feed our inner selves. To do so, we need to find meaning in what we do, and not just at work. That will allow us to live our lives with hope and enthusiasm.

Meaning

Vision and meaning are two concepts that are often confused. The vision and the meaning of work are not the same thing, although they go hand in hand. This is why we placed them in the same chapter: to make their relationship clearer and to explore how they are managed together.

> We who lived in concentration camps remember the men who walked through the huts comforting others, giving away their last piece of bread. They may be few in number, but they offer sufficient proof that everything can be taken from a man but one thing: the last of the human freedoms—to choose one's attitude in any given circumstances, to choose one's own way. (Frankl 1984)

What is it that made people in such a harsh environment, one so conducive to that survivalist ego, able to show generosity and concern for others? That tremendous evidence that Austrian psychiatrist Viktor Frankl saw firsthand in the World War II concentration camps brought him an answer: meaning. For those people, offering help to others had meaning because it gave them control over their own lives in a situation where they could barely hold on to it with the tips of their fingers.

Meaning is the key that opens the doors of acceptance and, as such, of learning and growth. When people see some meaning in a situation, it reduces dissonance and multiplies their capacity for control. In contrast, when we are trapped in a perspective devoid of meaning, our brain goes into defensive mode and increases stress. It diminishes creativity, our capacity for learning, and potential for identifying opportunities. We feel cornered with no way out.

Finding meaning in what we do requires us to answer one question: what for? It's incredibly hard to answer if we're being honest with ourselves and looking beyond the typical "to earn a living" or "because I need money for rent." So, why make the effort? Why leave your comfort zone? Why go beyond the superficial?

There are a lot of people who believe that work is just being at work, but don't know that is a personal decision: We can spend the same amount of hours either vegetating or using them as a possibility to grow and learn. In fact, we make that decision every day of our lives! And we can either do it consciously (and grow as professionals) or we can let life decide for us. Again, we can only manage what we're aware of; what we're unaware of manages us.

The simple act of opening people's minds to this fact often has magical effects on their attitude. Good leaders know it. They're able to make members of their team see that work is exactly what they want it to be because they decide how they will live it. Deep down, nobody wants to live like a robot.

I remember an experience from school that had a profound effect on me. In a French class, the teacher had to leave the room for a while and left us alone, but didn't leave anyone in charge to make sure the rest didn't goof off, as teachers usually did back then. An impressive amount of chaos gradually ensued, so much so that when the teacher returned, we couldn't rein it in and give even the impression of normalcy. I mean, he caught us red handed. Unfazed, he walked over to the chalkboard and wrote a single word in large letters: slaves. Then he sat in silence.

We were shocked. There was no yelling, no threats, and no punishment. Confusion turned to curiosity and we slowly quieted down. When the dust settled, the teacher said something that has stuck with me to this day: "You are slaves. You are here to learn and grow, but instead you need someone to threaten you with punishment to do so, rather than decide for yourselves how to behave." He then picked up where he left off with his lesson. We sat there pensively and for the rest of the class something floated around in the atmosphere. I don't think I exaggerate when I say that it was an air of transcendence. Suddenly, he had put us in touch with the meaning of what we were doing. He took us beyond the simple act of being there constrained in that place for a few hours a day. And he did all this almost without words. He did it with his attitude.

Of course, at that age, life passes lightly and we remained the mindless people we had been for years. But that event has come to mind many times since. The seed that my teacher planted in my memory has grown and now, nearly 40 years later, I can see the influence it's had on me. At work I have always tried to go above and beyond the task and make it an exercise in personal growth. I am convinced that it was all due to experiences like this one. It's fantastic when a teacher also turns out to be a leader!

Meaning and Results

Give me a stock clerk with a goal and I'll give you a man who will make history. Give me a man with no goals and I'll give you a stock clerk.

—James Cash Penney, American Entrepreneur and Businessman

When we find ourselves with an authoritarian boss who is often short on empathy and thinks all of this is just nonsense, he focuses on the tasks that make up the job and doesn't make sure that people understand and live the meaning of it. As a result, his people feel like cogs in a machine. They don't own the job and are unable to find any meaning in it whatsoever.

When people don't find meaning in what they have to do, instead of creating or constructing, according to Viktor Frankl, they often "do what others do (conformity) or do what others want them to do (totalitarianism)."

In fact, isn't that the dream of every authoritarian boss? Some even go so far as outright saying it: "You aren't here to think. You're here to do what I tell you to do." That's why minds shut down, stress intensifies, fear takes hold, and teams that are ordered around get used to responding worse to uncertainty than teams that are lead.

If you have had to live with an autocrat, finding meaning in your job could help you tolerate him. In the words of Friedrich Nietzsche, "If you know the why to living, you can tolerate any how." We could turn the phrase to say that without a "why," almost any "how" is intolerable.

How to Give Meaning

Once again, we find ourselves in a craftsman's challenge. To understand the how, let's look at Deborah Ancona's definition of *to give meaning*:

> To give meaning is the process by which individuals develop a profound understanding of the problem they seek to solve, which is essential for

change. People who give meaning understand the global context of their effort, how it's changing, and where it's headed so that, as they make a decision, they can do so with the larger context in mind. (Watt 2012)

For Ancona, creating meaning requires everyone involved to profoundly understand not just the job, but also its context. It seems like a very systemic perspective. They should live the project like something that transcends the tasks that make it up and accept that the project is alive and undergoing its own evolution. If we understand and look a bit further, we can also make decisions that preserve that meaning and easily accept necessary changes. I like to look at it like this: Instead of being responsible for tasks or functions, we become guardians of meaning!

If you want to lead projects (truly lead and not simply instruct or coordinate them), you should practice a more open communication style: Substitute the old, "information is power," for the new, "information is power when it's shared with the group." For people to understand the meaning behind a project, they must get information much sooner than they used to. You must manage information in a network openly so that everyone can analyze it, give their opinions, reach a consensus, manage conflicts constructively, and ultimately maintain the meaning of the project.

Meaning, Routine, and Creativity

In the absence of meaning, we hide behind routine to avoid the emptiness we feel. To avoid thinking, we drug ourselves with the task (what we're doing) and in that way obtain some sense of security or, at least, comfort. We end up experiencing changes like something that we don't understand (they mean nothing to us), we don't want to hear anything new, and we cling to what we know. That's how most resistance to change in business projects is born.

> It's spectacular how the attitudes of a project team change when they understand the meaning of the necessary changes! Assuming that those in charge haven't lost their credibility by not cluing people in when the time is right.

Businesses often invest time and money in workshops crafted by high-level (expensive) consultants to define their mission. But that poor old mission will probably end up posted online somewhere, sad and alone. The initial intent of those efforts was surely sincere, because the mission was designed to connect employees with their work. When it's achieved, the mission becomes a genuine management tool. However, that most likely isn't the case and we will see why.

For the mission to be really useful, every member of the company (managers are key here) should make themselves stewards of practicing it on a daily basis, despite any pressure for results, from stress, or from the market. It's not enough for them to know it. They have to live it and embody it. And here we find something important—everyone can find a different meaning in the same project:

> What matters isn't the meaning of life in general terms, but rather the specific meaning of a person's life in a given moment. (Frankl 1984)

The meaning of work is something very personal. That means that if you want to lead, you should work hard to know your team because it is your job to connect the project with the meaning that each individual may find in it. A leader must find the keys for that connection within each individual. It's a craftsman's effort, but if you pull it off, no leadership tool is more powerful.

Vision

Managing vision will make you a movie director! Vision is a movie (a visualization or mental image) of a successful future for the team that's so vivid and attractive that it makes you want to make it a reality.

The most direct way to generate a vision is to start by creating our own mental movie, in which we see ourselves and our team winning and getting what we want. The more detailed and lifelike you make it, the more powerful your vision will be, the more emotional connection you create, and the more inspired you will be to share it. As psychologist Abraham Maslow (1965) observed in highly effective business teams: "the task was no longer separate from the self, but rather he identified with the task so strongly that he couldn't define his real self without including that task."

If you become possessed by your vision, if you live it intensely, you will breathe authenticity, and, as a result, your credibility and ability to influence the team will be tremendous. Remember that leadership is formed and flows on an emotional level: Live your dream intensely so that others can live it too.

> Your movie should have a message: We're moving toward that future and we're starting now. The hike will be fueled by connecting that vision with the meaning of our work.

In fact, this is the only reason for this vision to exist—to tell us how we're going to dream the mission, how we'll live it, and how we'll shape the dream in our reality. As we have seen, when we're connected with our work, it is transformed to become part of the essence of our lives. Not only are we more creative and productive, but we also enjoy doing it.

Otherwise, that same job becomes an obligation that we need to live our real lives, which is what we do outside work. Lots of people feel this way and that is why we get, what I call, Friday flight. This is when everybody bolts out of the office at the end of the week, stressed out, like bats out of hell, fleeing from desks and workshops. Many companies semiconsciously go along with it by letting their employees drop their masks a bit; I'm referring, of course, to casual Friday.

It's remarkable how our level of commitment can vary from one case to another. When vision connects us with meaning, what we do helps us to grow, but without it, we whither. As writer, consultant, and filmmaker Robert Fritz once said, "In the presence of greatness, pettiness disappears." But we can add, in the absence of a great dream pettiness prevails.

For Peter Senge (1990), although adaptive learning (born of reaction) is possible without a vision, generative learning (born of conscious creation) is only possible when people work to reach something they feel deeply connected to. The idea of generative learning—expanding our ability to create—is abstract and superficial unless people are motivated by a vision: With a genuine vision in place, people don't learn because they're ordered to do so, but because they want to.

That's why it's so important not to confuse a vision with an objective. Objectives are necessary and useful, but they rarely ever elicit the emotions, creativity, and motivations needed to build something new. An objective speaks to our rational mind. A vision speaks to our emotion. An objective is monitored while vision is lived. A true vision should get us to look within, to find and mobilize our own standards for excellence.

Why Vision Fails

We now know that vision is born of a dream. How many dreams were born of cold, rational thought? Usual planning methods, like traditional "vision development" workshops, can be quite useful when it comes to establishing objectives, but they don't lead to truly effective visions. Instead, these visions are cold and not very motivational, so much so that I'd go as far as calling them "orthopedic." Orthopedics are used to correct deformities, intervening in the body externally and by force. If we analyze the reasons why traditional vision development workshops fail, we'll understand the analogy better:

- The vision in question comes from commitments and negotiations between the interests of the participants, in which calculation is often used rather than empathy and a communal sensibility. When logic and reasoning reign, emotions don't just disappear; it's as if they never existed. I wouldn't recommend eliminating reason altogether, but we can't just jettison emotions either. Emotions are what move people. We have to align both of these elements and, of course, we now know that first we feel, then we think.

- In traditional workshops, logic is present throughout the whole process; creation often involves challenging the unknown and sometimes even logic itself. This is especially true when we talk about disruptive innovation because it's very hard to imagine the potential of something that has no precedent. For example, when Steve Wozniak and Steve Jobs created the first personal computer, they went to Hewlett-Packard, the company with which Wozniak had a relationship. As we know, Hewlett-Packard rejected them because "why would anyone want a computer in their home?" And we're talking about a highly innovative company!

- To accept the new, our mind has to grab onto some concept that offers a mental support or bridge. For example, in the early days of the automobile market, automobiles were often presented as "horseless carriages" because that was the mental anchor people used to understand such a novel concept. In fact, we still call them cars (rather than automobiles) to this day.

- When vision arises as the solution to a problem or a response to a specific situation, once the problem goes away or the situation changes, the energy that you had mobilized will also go away. It's the "we don't need it anymore" effect, which is an unequivocal signal that the vision wasn't properly grounded in meaning, because meaning rarely changes with its circumstances.

- Vision that comes from a classical consulting workshop is created by a small group of higher-ups who think about what's good for the organization (everyone else will have to live it in the flesh). It's then communicated to managers of varying hierarchy to be implanted. At which point in the process does the dream die? How can you connect that process with the specific meaning that I may find in my work?

Visions are obtained from the outside, people in the organization receive them passively, and they are left with the task of *making them their own*. Formulations drafted by the managers completely ignore the personal visions of others (sometimes even their very own), which are sacrificed on the altar of the strategic vision or the official vision of "the folks upstairs." In these circumstances, vision is not lived, but tolerated. Some vision that is!

When vision becomes orthopedic, commitment isn't achieved with the same intensity and we can't use it as a management tool to energize the group. Peter Senge (1990) helps us clarify the different ways people respond to a vision:

- **Commitment.** We want the vision and are ready to go. We will do whatever's necessary.

- **Enlistment.** We want the vision and will do what's possible within the spirit of the law.

- **Genuine compliance.** We see the benefits of the vision and will do what's expected of us and more, as the norm dictates. We will be good soldiers.

- **Formal compliance.** We see the benefits of the vision and will do what's expected of us, but nothing more.

- **Reluctant compliance.** We don't see the benefits of the vision, but we don't want to lose our jobs. We'll do enough to keep us from being punished because we have no other options, but we definitely feel marginalized.

- **Disobedience.** We don't see the benefits of the vision and won't do what's expected of us.

- **Apathy.** We're neither for nor against the vision. We have neither the interest nor the energy to engage. "We don't care. It's not our fight."

Gain Commitment Using Vision

How can you get people to commit? In a way, we've already hinted at it, but let's lay it out more explicitly:

1. Create a mental movie that is vivid and full of detail, including those that may be seen, by you or others, as negative or dangerous. With hope and without fear.

2. Live it intensely in your mind and feel it in your heart.

3. Start personally putting it into practice regularly. Before you describe it to others, lead by example. Let others look at you strangely and let them see the vision giving you a new kind of energy.

4. Explain the vision. Linger on the details to help make it more vivid and sincere. Don't leave anything out, including those aspects that your team may deem negative. Don't be a salesman, be a missionary: Your credibility should come from your authenticity, not your argument.

5. Give the vision over to your team. Let them get their hands on it, live it, and share it. Encourage them to enrich the vision by adding their own details. Let them give it wings so that it can take flight. Remember that your intention is to convert your vision into their vision, so keep an open mind: the shared vision will probably be richer and more powerful, even if it's not identical to your original one. Remember that as a leader, you work for them.

10

Managing Values

Try not to become a man of success, but a man of value.

—Albert Einstein, *Einstein and the Poet*

A proud man is always looking down on things and people; and, of course, as long as you are looking down, you cannot see something that is above you.

—C.S. Lewis, *Mere Christianity*

The Role of Values in a Team

In a practical way, we can define values as mental states that determine our nature and guide our conduct. They are the source of our internal energy and they manifest themselves through emotions that determine how we live a situation: When some value is honored by our actions, our energy goes up, we seem to vibrate, and we enter into resonance. On the contrary, if something tramples a value we find relevant, we feel dissonance—we feel bad, our energy drops, and, if the situation is prolonged, we could even suffer from stress.

We find the same happens in teams. From a systemic perspective we have seen that the team is like a supra-personality (a personality made up of personalities plus the relationships created between them), and it's possible to establish a perfect analog. In this case values are also the source of resonance and dissonance, and, as a result, properly managing them is fundamental to developing leadership.

It's not necessary for all members of the group to have the exact same values, as long as they share enough certain common ones. We call these team values and they constitute the glue of your corporate culture. They determine what your team considers good or bad, and what behaviors are deemed correct and incorrect. This common value framework is the main difference between being a true team and just a group of people: Without shared values, the team ceases to be a team.

This may or may not be a conscious process. Only in the first case, when the team knows what their values are, is proactive management possible. Let's remember again that we manage what we're aware of. What we're not aware of manages us. So building a conscious value framework that is shared among the team and actively strengthening it is essential to good leadership.

Recognizing the Existing Group Values

But what happens when you find yourself with the challenge of leading an established team, one that has already solidified their prior values, dynamics, and habits? This case is similar to climbing aboard a moving train: First you need to gain speed, jump up to a train car, and then quickly find your seat. By now you know that it's a fairly common situation—you are put in charge, but still need to earn your leadership—and one of your first steps should be to find out which values motivate the team.

Whatever your intention, you will have to start by understanding the pre-existing foundation, what's already there. If you start making changes without taking that into account, you risk being the proverbial bull in the china shop that makes a big mess of things. Good management starts by knowing and accepting the facts. Value management comes from emotional energy and belongs more to leadership than to power. At this point, you have the latter, but still have to earn the former. Changing values by force is traumatic and always ends up being surgical: People don't resist change, rather they resist being changed.

Therefore, it behooves you to make the effort to uncover which values rule over the team and, more importantly, how each member of the team lives them. You can achieve this by becoming an attentive observer of the behaviors that people value as positive and negative: what makes them vibrate, what annoys them, and what "turns them off" to the job.

You will probably find that they're OK with lots of values, but maybe not with how they're implemented. Often, problems don't come from the value itself, but rather the behavior that's associated with it, or even which value should take priority over a contradicting one. For example, hiding a mistake to protect a coworker could be considered part of the value of solidarity. However, it would contradict the value of accountability, and, even with the best of intentions, members of the team might not know how to deal with it. The criteria necessary to distinguish and prioritize values are often called the value scale or hierarchy. Creating such criteria is also the leader's job.

> The most important role of values is in the day-to-day minutiae,
> dealing with specific behaviors, and in prioritizing one value over
> another, more so than in the list of values itself.

Putting Values to Work

The best use of values comes from leadership: If you feel ready to use them, dive right into it. No one else will tell you when you're ready. When you have identified the eight or nine values that are most important to the group (and their order of priority) you can start to decide which ones you'd like to change and how to prioritize them. By contrast, when you put together a group from scratch, you can build the referential value framework as if on a blank canvas.

One way or another, now you will take your next step: building the right value framework so that the team functions the way you think it should. At this point, you'll face an exciting dilemma: Is it better to propose your own idea to the group or have them create that framework together as a team? The answer will come as much from the situation (and how urgently you need to make decisions) as from your own management style.

In order for the values to have their beneficial effects on the team, they must be accepted, adopted, and shared by everyone. Creating the value framework as a group with your team favors this process. That said, as the one ultimately responsible for the team, you have every right to establish the value framework you think is most beneficial. Don't doubt that for a second. In any event, you'll have to get them to accept it, adopt it, and share it. You can't just impose it on them. Communicate it genuinely. Live it as something essential. Convey your own conviction. From that moment, your guiding reference is, again, once the value framework is defined, everyone on the team should accept it, adopt it, share it, and, above all, commit to it. The implications are very important: Whoever doesn't should leave the team.

People who demonstrate behavior that substantially threatens the group's values will have an enormously negative impact on the others: They will be a constant affirmation that the value framework (the rules of the game that everyone has adopted) is written in the sand and will ridicule those who honor it. "If that person can step all over our values whenever they like, why can't I?" That person will also put your influence as a leader into question. It's a true cancer for the team. Metastasis is just a matter of time.

We should be emphatic on this point because it deals with a crucial aspect that we will deal with extensively. It's also related to the question,

"Why are an organization's values posted online, ignored, and forgotten by everyone, or hung in dusty frames in some sad corner of the office next to the coffee machine?" What a sad (and telling) way to go!

Once the value framework is established, the team's behavior should reflect it. As a leader, you should develop a permanent pedagogy relating the team's behavior with the corresponding values. This will be a significant part of your leadership role. To this end, you will have just three tools:

- **Example.** We've seen the importance of personal influence based on authority, and that's precisely where it's most evident. As a leader, you can only demand from others that which you are willing to do, and they will require you to act accordingly. You can't ask them to practice accountability if they see you show up late to a meeting in the morning looking hungover. This is the main reason that values fall by the wayside: managers' inability to practice what they demand of others. Make no mistake, you must become a living example, the highest proponent of the values you wish to promote, their faithful guardian. And furthermore, you'll have to do it consistently. Remember that you're teaching these things and teaching requires repetition.

- **Recognition.** Human beings respond much better to positive reinforcement than to punishment. Every time (and I mean every time) that someone on your team does something that honors a value, put it on display before the group and congratulate that person publicly. They will all take notice. But always remember that you should direct your praise toward the behavior more than the person and relate it with the value or values that you have seen: "Good job helping your coworker because on this team we want to be supportive of one another." If you don't do this, it's less effective. The impact that recognition has on us is much greater when it's directed at something that we've done because it's concrete, tangible, and drives us to repeat it. In many organizations, people think that they only need to point out the bad stuff because the good stuff should be the norm. And they ignore recognition's enormous motivational potential. People don't work that way. We need positive reinforcement.

- **Constructive criticism.** When a behavior goes against one of the team's values, make it clear by telling that person publicly, exposing the behavior, not the person. Constructive criticism differs from toxic criticism in this way: The person should not feel attacked because then they'll focus on defending themselves and not on learning. In contrast, emphasize your confidence in that person. Then highlight in what way that behavior goes against a value, directing their attention toward finding alternative behaviors that are in line with those values. Show how they can apply those behaviors the next time they are faced with a similar situation. To give constructive criticism effectively you should stay focused on the task and never act defensively from your ego ("how could you do this to me?").

With Values, There Are No Trivial Subjects

Building values requires knowing the importance of seemingly insignificant situations. It's important to bear in mind that in developing values, we also educate (or sometimes, miseducate) by omission.

On an emotional level, humans are like cars with an automatic transmission, lacking a clutch, just a brake and gas pedal. There is no middle ground. If a negative behavior is ignored because "I can't deal with it right now," "it happens in other teams," or "it's not a big deal," you're unintentionally acting against that value by effectively sanctioning it and thus establishing a precedent. Albeit subconsciously.

Many managers have difficulty with this ("I'm so busy that I can't be on top of everything") without realizing that they're taking a big risk with their authority and, by extension, their team. Experience has shown me countless situations where trivial acts have the most symbolic value. This poses a great challenge for any busy executive because it demands time (and self-management) for subjects that, according to traditional business school criteria, are not a priority.

But it makes sense: Important issues make people drag their feet and we don't show who we really are; in contrast, little things relax us and allow us to open up. That's where their symbolic power comes from. I've seen all-out wars fought over a window or a ficus, that's why they're perfect fodder for teaching about values. Don't undervalue or waste a single one.

11

Managing Beliefs, Assumptions, and Prejudices

It's easier to break an atom than a prejudice.

—Albert Einstein

Beliefs and Belief Systems

Just as we have a skeleton that supports and structures our body, our thoughts have their own skeleton that shapes them. We call this a belief system. Beliefs are convictions that determine and modulate our thought patterns, which are created primarily during early childhood. They are the source of assumptions and prejudices that will determine the way we think and feel. In short, they condition our attitude and decision making.

Beliefs aren't there by chance. They are the product of what we learn when, in the process of developing our character, we face the outside world—which in our early years primarily means family. Therefore, these beliefs have been useful in past experiences.

However, a greater rate of change and global complexity make it ever more likely that a belief that we once found useful will turn into an obstacle, which we then refer to as a limiting belief. In the past, human life was shorter and the world was less likely to change. Our belief system was relatively unchallenged over the course of our lives. That's why we haven't been brought up to modify it. But this has become a necessity in facing the uncertainty that absorbs us—an uncertainty that comes from accelerated change and growing complexity.

What can we do about a belief that's become limiting? You can't eliminate it, but you can exchange it for another one. Thus the strategy consists of learning to modify our belief system by substituting limiting beliefs for non-limiting ones.

The main problem is in our awareness of when we're being affected by a limiting belief. Beliefs owe their power, in large part, to operating in the subconscious. Remember that we can manage what we're aware of. What we're not aware of, manages us. This makes it difficult—if not impossible—to willingly change our belief system without outside help, for example, from a professional coach.

There are very basic beliefs in our personality, such as "if I'm not complacent, they won't like me" or "if you're too demanding, you end up alone." These are hard to change because they're rooted deeply and we're hardly even aware of them. Other beliefs, such as "men don't cry" or "to succeed in life, you need to be a homeowner," are part of the culture we live in.

Just like people, organizations and teams also create beliefs; they are responsible for so-called groupthink, which, when it starts to limit internal evaluation, could become the dark side of the organization's culture.

Beliefs and the Comfort Zone

Our belief system draws an imaginary boundary that defines the comfort zone: It is shaped by all the emotional characteristics and thoughts (and even habits) that we accept of ourselves and which rarely question our belief system; they neither challenge nor test it. As the name indicates, when we act within our comfort zone, we feel comfortable. We don't have to exert ourselves much and we take things easy. We feel secure, but often we also feel conformist and limited. In summary, when we're in our comfort zone, we "do things," but learn very little.

> Challenge, adventure, and real growth live in that uncharted territory that exists beyond the horizon. Relevant learning demands that we immerse ourselves in the unknown, do different things—or do things differently—and it challenges us to assume the risks it implies.

Real learning is found outside your comfort zone. Crossing that border, we are inundated with feelings of fear and insecurity. These signals warn us that we're entering into unknown territory. Accept them! When we're open to adventure and listen closely we can hear more . . . they don't come alone! These signals come in the good company of hope and excitement. We're alive!

If we thrust ourselves into proactively confronting adventure, we'll see that the reward is truly great, regardless of the end result. We learn a great deal this way; we feel like we've grown and we find that this creates an enormous sense of completeness. We become motivated and gain the courage to take on new challenges. In contrast, if we shrink before the prospect of adventure, we feel smaller and less powerful; our comfort zone becomes our prison.

As a result, learning to step decisively out of your comfort zone empowers your personal leadership, which projects onto others and spreads that attitude throughout the team. In this way, leadership encourages the team to take chances, dare to question themselves, and take risks that they can learn from. It's part of the essence of a leadership style known as coach, which is fundamental in creating a corporate culture based on learning, flexibility, and creativity.

So that's all well and good when we voluntarily seek out adventure, but how often do we find ourselves dragged outside our comfort zone by life when we don't want to be? What happens in these circumstances? Whether a difficult work situation, joblessness, or illness, life constantly puts us in situations that challenge our comfort zone and toss us outside it. We can—and should—choose what attitude we'll take on in these situations, as Viktor Frankl has shown us. In this case, we've sought it out willingly, but we can still decide to accept it and evolve from it, resist it, shut it out, or accept it in theory, but not in practice—that is, resign ourselves to it.

I've had the opportunity to do a lot of work with entrepreneurs. I've seen how different that path is and how different the results are between those who do it out of a passion for starting a business and those who do it because they want a job "like I used to have" or "one that suits them better." In the former case, proactivity surges like a force of nature. The latter begins from a place of resignation and leads only to constant stress—what new project can possibly end well when we ultimately don't want to do it? Again, we're reminded of Carl Jung: "what you resist, persists and what you accept, changes." Only true acceptance will make us capable of turning the situation into a learning opportunity and a creative space.

> The ability to evolve and learn from any human collective will correlate to how you cultivate your capacity to venture outside your comfort zone, modify your belief system, and question your assumptions.

Beliefs and Assumptions

The organization's beliefs—things like "there's nothing left to invent in this company," "meetings are a waste of time," and "showing emotion is a sign of weakness"—originate from assumptions. Some of the assumptions that may lead to these beliefs include, "don't bother going above and beyond on new projects," "nothing productive will actually come out of this meeting," or "he isn't strong enough to lead this team." These will undoubtedly affect decision making and interpersonal relationships.

These assumptions happen automatically and subconsciously. Leaders should be on the lookout for assumptions—beginning with their own—in order to challenge them and navigate the team toward finding more open points of view. As a general rule, assumptions don't hold up well to rational analysis rooted in facts, as long as it's done with the utmost respect. If it's not, members of the team will feel personally assaulted and will go on the defensive. To do this well, the leader must know how to separate objectives—data—from the emotional impact that they can provoke. And in this case, authority will come from your demonstrated capacity to question your own beliefs, that is, to apply the same criteria to yourself as you do to your team.

Thus managing beliefs means constantly questioning assumptions, so that you can distinguish *knowing* from *assuming you know*. This is much easier when it's done as a team, when people help to keep each other in check. One key to success for high-functioning teams is their ability to question themselves constantly. If this behavior isn't developed, it's impossible to establish a learning culture within an organization. Lastly, we should stress the importance of sustained effort in the face of constant temptation for a team to get comfortable. Therefore, the effort to maintain that questioning is no less important than actually achieving it!

12

Managing Expectations and Modifying Perspectives

A man is made mortal by his fears, and immortal by his desires.

—Pythagoras

What the caterpillar calls the end of the world,
the master calls a butterfly.

—Richard Bach, *Illusions*

We know that before action comes the desire to act. That desire to undertake an action—or avoid one—is called attitude and is fueled by the emotional energy of what we're actively experiencing. Attitude comes from how we live a certain situation. We also know that active thought rarely plays a role in this: We live the majority of our lives mentally reaching back into the past recovering information (remembering) and into the future making predictions (seeing before an action takes place) with the goal of preventing dangers and difficulties. This happens because our brain is a powerful survival machine. To survive, our species has relied heavily on that capacity to get ahead of the threats. Considering how much we have proliferated, our success in this area is clear, at least, so far.

So, we should think of the brain as a "prediction factory." It's constantly playing out probable future outcomes as if they were Hollywood films, most of which happens subconsciously. However we imagine that the future is how we want to act. This mechanism is so powerful that our first instinct is always to make events fit into the prediction that they have led us to create: Have you ever been in a situation where you see only what you want to see? It's only at second glance, when the facts are stubborn, that we stop to revise our prediction. And the greater our emotional attachment to what we've imagined, the more we cling to it! So much so that, as the popular saying goes, "we refuse to see what's right under our nose."

There is a lot of research to suggest that we are the creators of our own reality. As the famous Chilean authors Humberto Maturana and Francisco Varela have said, "As regards human cognitive structures, the whole world of our experiences is within us, there is no such thing as an outside experience."

For centuries now, we have believed that observation precedes knowledge: We've believed that we see things as they are and then we give them a name. However, many researchers, among them Rafael Echeverría and Maturana, have concluded that, on the contrary, "one doesn't talk about what he sees, but rather sees that which he can talk about." It's our internal framework that defines how we see the external. Our brain is not designed for wisdom, but for survival. And to that end it has equipped us with glasses that skew our vision to support what, as a function of our past history as a species—and I stress *past*—we have determined will help us survive. That's why self-deception is part of our essence as people.

In 1964, Robert Rosenthal, then a young social psychology professor at Harvard, began a famous experiment: The result of his study, published in 1968 and entitled *Pygmalion in the Classroom*, gave rise to what is now known as the Pygmalion Effect or the Rosenthal Effect. It proposed that people who have positive expectations of their children, students, or collaborators generate a warmer socio-emotional environment and give more and better feedback, which has a positive effect on their development.

In Greek mythology, Pygmalion was a prince from Cyprus who grew tired searching for the perfect woman, and finally decided to sculpt a model out of ivory instead. Every day he would mold her in the image of what, to his mind, a perfect woman should be. He finally completed a figure so beautiful that it surpassed his own imagination. He named it Galatea. The sculpture was so gorgeous that he wound up falling in love with it. Seeing this, the goddess Venus brought the statue to life, making Pygmalion's dream into a reality. The term Pygmalion Effect is used to describe how the judgment, desire, and fear we have about people, things, situations, and even ourselves, have the tendency to become realities.

Rosenthal began his experiment administering an intelligence test to a group of students from a pre-selected school. He then divided the group into two categories at random. He told the teacher of the first group (the control group) that her group contained average students; however, the teacher of the second group (the experimental group) was told that her students were above average and that she could expect accelerated progress from them. Obviously, this distinction was completely false.

At the end of the course, Rosenthal returned to administer the test to the students. The results showed that the students falsely described as highly advanced had improved much more than the control group. Even though both groups had previously been equal, the expectations that Rosenthal had created in their teachers were very different. In collaboration with Lenore Jacobson, director of the school, Rosenthal discovered the following: Teachers who believed that a student was good, smiled at that student more often, looked them in the eyes more, gave them more feedback—regardless of whether their answers were correct—and their praise was much clearer. By telling teachers that certain students were exceptional, Rosenthal modified their expectations of those students, leading them subconsciously to behave in a way that promoted their students' success. The Pygmalion Effect is also known as a self-fulfilling prophesy: When we desire or fear something, we increase the probability that it will come true.

This also happens between a leader and his team: Whether or not you're aware of it, leaders are managers of expectations. For example, as we've already seen, when a leader proposes a vision to his team, he's trying to generate a set of expectations that will predispose his team to behave how he prefers. That way the impulse for action will come from within each person, while increasing the commitment to the project. For this reason, managing expectations is one of the fundamental keys of leadership.

Although it's often mentioned anecdotally, to fulfill an ISO requirement, or simply to follow the trend, the real essence of a vision is to create expectations that drive the team toward the achievement of their goals, ensuring they commit, and remain committed and proactive even when things get really tough. Once again, we find ourselves in the midst of the emotional energy that keeps the gears in motion.

> The expectation is reinforced by the emotional magma that's formed by sharing values within a team, its systemic personality, and the lessons learned by the sum of its experiences. These elements are a significant part of what we call the team's (or the organization's) corporate culture and they ultimately condition our perception of a possible or desirable future.

What is the mechanism? Similar to how we view events individually, the human system, which behaves like a supra-entity—an individual made up of individuals—also constructs its own belief structure, which dictates what we cannot or should not do. Here, too, this can essentially be interpreted as a combination of the fears and hopes that the team faces: They're the brakes and gas pedals of the team's emotional machinery when they put their mission into action.

From a systemic perspective, we could think of expectation as the resulting form of the combination of effort to drive the team to advance or retreat. And this result will give rise to the way in which the team experiences that situation—their attitude.

How the Leader Should Manage Expectations

The first step a leader should take in managing expectations of any team is obvious: Know what the team's expectations are at that moment. He should start by knowing which emotions they're feeling, and then work back from there until it's clear what expectations the team created about the situation. The team creates these emotions and then hides behind them.

For example, fear can come from the expectation of punishment when something goes wrong, which is based on the assumption that "in this company, the price for mistakes is high." Frustration can also come from our expecting to get praise for something we deem worthy, but that our superiors don't acknowledge.

The second step consists of normalizing these expectations—making everyone aware of them—as we'll see later. Remember that what we're aware of is manageable. What we're unaware of manages us. Once you have clear expectations you should ask the team a question: "Is this how we truly want to live this situation?"

The third step is even more demanding and requires more commitment: Have additional expectations that you can propose to the group as alternatives. This is very important: Leadership doesn't stop at what is—that would simply be administration—but rather goes beyond that to decidedly inhabit what could be. This and only this is the meaning of leadership: to direct the group toward that possibility. A leader can come up with these alternate expectations in one of two ways, which aren't necessarily incompatible:

- Come up with new perspectives on the situation, which is often referred to as developing a vision, and in this way embody the most sought-after leadership style, the visionary leader. We've already learned how to create a vision.

- Collect new perspectives that other members of the team create, but aren't able to promote on their own—either due to lack of authority or communication skills. Remember that the role of the leader means ensuring that energy and ideas flow throughout the group, regardless of who creates them.

As a fourth step, leaders should embody the new perspectives they defend sincerely, believing in them, and feeling them as a part of themselves. We've seen that being genuine is necessary to be believable. We cannot expect others to believe if we don't believe; when leaders don't believe in what they're promoting, they become mere manipulators. But if leaders honestly believe and defend those beliefs completely, their conviction will permeate through their non-verbal communication and will create the emotional base necessary to carry their message.

13

Trust

We have seen the effect that leadership has on an emotional level: Good and bad leadership is felt. For this reason, in order for good leadership to be present, you need a solid base of self-awareness from the leader and a solid emotional connection between members of the group. You can't achieve that without believing in yourself and the people on your team. Let's test this theory with two real life examples of what happens when trust is missing:

A Real Experience

We held a meeting in a comfortable hotel meeting room with the most prestigious members of the advertising agency that handled the majority of our accounts. Our company was considered a major advertiser and, in the face of accelerated changes in our sector, we set up this meeting to revise our communication strategy. It's a very important subject and we were relying on our boss to be there.

At some point, my new assistant made a brilliant comment. Without thinking, I took a piece of paper, wrote down "excellent comment," and passed it to him. He looked at it and smiled, but the boss noticed. Immediately, from the other side of the long meeting table he disregarded the immersive debate taking place around him, and asked for the paper directly. Everyone looked up. My assistant, who was relatively new to the company, got bright red with embarrassment and handed it over. The boss read it, raised an eyebrow, and stared at me disgusted. I held firmly until he broke away.

What happened? By the look on his face, he was either thinking "what a silly thing to do" or "what is Cuervo thinking?" What he was surely not aware of was how his behavior had affected the others in the room.

Another Real Experience

We had a new "boss's boss." In an effort to motivate us, he decided to take us to a sales convention in Paris. A classic formula: some work, mixed with sight-seeing that business partners could even bring their spouses along on.

In his inaugural action, the "boss's boss" gave his motivational speech. It started well enough, but dragged on and his true self started to peak through: In a spectacular crescendo, he shifted from professing his profound confidence in the team to making us aware of the difficulties of the market, and ending with threatening to fire everyone if we didn't meet the objectives he would demand of us at this convention. The room goes cold—from euphoria to a glacial finale.

After the "boss's boss" finished his speech, we in the marketing department talked about the year's latest news. Our enthusiasm was frozen and with it, the audience's response. When I finished my speech, I walked by the "boss's boss" and he told me, "Cuervo, the marketing department isn't motivating our business partners." I replied, "It's no surprise. You just threatened to fire each and every one of us." He stared at me surprised: He didn't realize what he'd done!

Inspiring Confidence Is Believing

You now know that in the arena of leadership you won't find "techniques to manipulate others into doing what you want them to do." This simply isn't possible. You cannot learn leadership techniques without committing to them deeply—they won't work. Making others change without you changing doesn't belong to leadership; it belongs to commanding, to being a boss!

> A fundamental part of learning from leadership is learning to trust in
> yourself and in others, regardless of how much uncertainty you have
> to swallow. To lead, you have to be exposed, you have to dive into the
> deep end, and firmly believe that others will respond to your message,
> even though you'll never be certain of it.

But don't worry if you can't do this. Remember being a good boss is already, in and of itself, a big step. A fair boss with solid standards can benefit the development of the team, although that person won't directly act as a leader. Make no mistake, this is how things are. Or go ahead and lie to yourself: Deploy that ego and convince yourself that they're all just ingrates who don't get it or, better yet, they're stupid. Obviously, if you've chosen this path, by now you've realized that this isn't the book for you and in all probability you haven't even stuck around to read these lines.

Let's stay on track and remember the central theme of this chapter: What is the relationship between trust and leadership and why is it so important? As you may recall, the meaning of leadership is to bring people from simply *doing* to *wanting to do*. That way, they'll bring their entire selves to bear on the work, including their hearts and minds. That will increase their commitment and motivation, which are essential when facing uncertainty.

> Have no doubt: If your organization's results depend on innovation,
> flexibility, creativity, or client service, you need leadership. These
> abilities are fundamentally based on attitude, and leadership comes
> from people's attitudes.

In order to be innovative, to sense opportunities, to find creative solutions, or simply to withstand the pressure without biting each other's heads off, we need an open mind that is committed to trying and learning. And for that we must trust our superiors and colleagues. If that trust isn't there, we won't dare to even try, put ourselves out there, or risk everything going wrong as we thought it would. Without that, there can be no learning.

Failure only happens when we decide that we've failed. As long as we stand up one more time after we're knocked down, we're still in the game. As Thomas Alva Edison said, "I have not failed. I've just found 10,000 different ways that won't work." Learning requires learning to fail well.

If we achieve learning that allows us to try alternate approaches, there is no true failure. And that means that people must truly believe that the organization will also share this value: There is no more destructive cancer for a team than thinking that our teammates can use our shortcomings—born of our desire to improve, innovate, and learn—to gain personal advantages at our expense because this kills trust. A team without trust doesn't evolve, it doesn't grow; it is already dead, it just doesn't know it yet. You want to destroy a team? All you have to do is sow mistrust and suspicion between its members.

We've seen that our brain has modes of operation, one that's proactive, creative, and constructive, in which hope and wanting to do prevail; and another that's reactive and defensive, which is clearly geared toward avoidance behaviors—fight, flight, or freezing up. If you lose trust in your teammates, you feel alone and the feeling of uncertainty will be more prevalent. Your brain will switch to its defensive mode and start to think of itself over the good of the team, saving its own behind.

Mistrust inspires so-called toxic relationship behaviors, which are the four types of relationship weapons that all humans, without exception, can use to defend themselves and assault their interpersonal relationships. They have been defined and studied extensively by John Gottman, psychologist at the University of Washington, who named them the Four Horsemen of the Apocalypse for Relationships:

- **Stonewalling:** closing yourself off to others, refusing to engage in dialogue, emotional withdrawal.

- **Defensiveness:** perceiving everything as a threat and seeing double meaning in it.
- **Criticism:** relieving yourself of responsibility by finding fault in others.
- **Contempt:** destructively criticizing others, disqualifying, and looking down on them.

These toxic behaviors are contagious and feed off of each other through members of the team. They create an atmosphere in which sincere debate and the search for solutions have no place. This begins a vicious circle that could, in the extreme, lead to the self-destruction of the team! You can see this process laid out in Figure 13-1.

FIGURE 13-1. THE CONSEQUENCES OF MISTRUST IN A TEAM

Adapted from Lencioni (2002).

Every good manipulator knows that, with a little skill, torpedoing a project is the perfect crime. You don't have to do anything, just increase uncertainty and sow mistrust so that toxic behaviors poison the relationships within the group. That will lead to mistakes that allow the manipulator to create a feeling of failure, which in turn will allow him to sow more toxic behavior. The rest is only a matter of time; when the pressure is on and uncertainty bites down, only solid leadership can avoid such a diabolical process. Unfortunately, it's common for those manipulators who follow the saying "troubled waters, fisherman's gain" to thrive. When something is supported by a proverb, it's already a part of our culture! In contrast, strengthening trust in oneself and others is the basis of efficiency and effectiveness. But what is trust really?

Genuine Trust

Direct professional experience has shown me that it's easy to confuse trust with joking around, laughing together, and, in short, having a good working environment. That is important, but it is not the kind of genuine trust that really matters!

> Real trust, the kind that really works, only exists when people are able to show their own vulnerabilities, not before then. You will have found it when, without fear of the consequences, you can tell your teammates things like "that's all I know," "I'm afraid," or "what you did hurt me."

It's what, on one occasion, a client brilliantly defined as true sincerity, which is a very powerful concept, hidden behind an apparent redundancy. It seems like a very fortunate expression that means to go beyond simple jokes to say what needs to be said! Or, in other words, the team getting along is often nothing but a smoke screen, a way to hide what we wouldn't dare lay out on the table. Speaking of true sincerity causes us to take a good look at ourselves: Are we really a sincere team? When sincerity is genuine, you don't need add-ons, just like with a good cup of coffee.

So what should a leader do?

Promote Real Trust

Something that is simple to understand, but not easy to put into practice is to put yourself out there. Or, what in this case is the same thing, lead by example. To promote real trust, you have to trust others!

If, in a difficult situation, you are able to show your own vulnerability in front of others, you'll be pleasantly surprised about the impact that it has. You'll see that the true origin of strength is in vulnerability. They are two sides of the same coin, although you'll have to challenge some of your own inner demons to achieve this.

> When a leader demonstrates vulnerability to others in a difficult situation, he opens the door to encourage others to do the same.

Great leaders know and practice it. That's why their strength, their influence on others, is based on discovering and accepting their own fears and limitations and putting themselves out on the line. If you do this, you will show your authenticity, the authority that is recognized by others. Of course, this requires that you believe in yourself and others because you won't have any guarantee that the team will respond. Remember that you cannot lead others without first leading yourself.

Put your vulnerability and doubts out there for others to see and do so genuinely. If you're pretending, you'll be found out in mere milliseconds! Humans have the most sensitive detectors for that sort of thing. If you do it sincerely, you'll be surprised by the impact you'll have. And when someone proposes their own vulnerability, support them and give them the recognition they deserve. You'll develop an awareness of how important it is to do this within your team and, paradoxically, that will make them feel more secure.

Remember that leading is believing:

- Believing in yourself: to put yourself out there genuinely, with the conviction that it will impact others.
- Believing in others: to trust that they'll be able to follow your lead and find their own way.

There are no guarantees that you'll get the result you're looking for, but your conviction will amplify the likelihood of success.

Want to foster trust in your team? Trust them! As John F. Kennedy said, "The only thing we have to fear is fear itself." The trust that you plant will be the foundation for healthy management, as seen in Figure 13-2.

FIGURE 13-2. HOW RESULTS ARE BUILT ON A TEAM

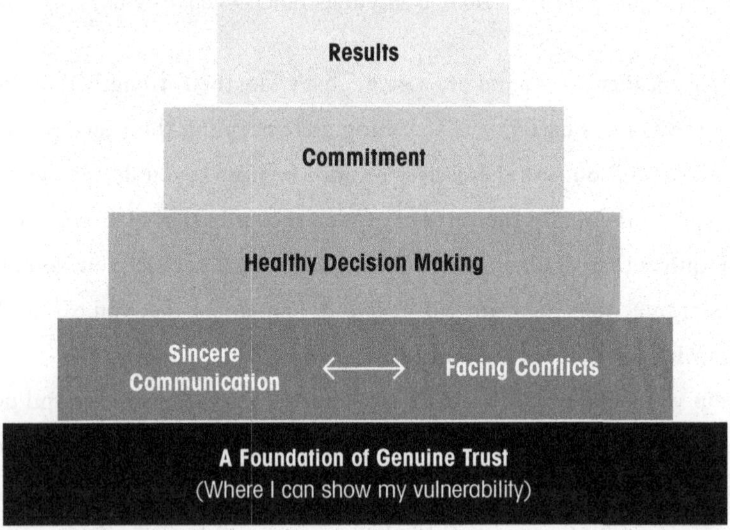

Results

Commitment

Healthy Decision Making

Sincere Communication ⟷ **Facing Conflicts**

A Foundation of Genuine Trust
(Where I can show my vulnerability)

Adapted from Lencioni (2002).

The process will be:

1. If you achieve trust, members of the team won't fear saying what they have to say and will face disagreements constructively, while diminishing the fear of conflict.

2. By diminishing fear of conflict, communication will be more sincere, fluid, and effective because people will say what needs to be said and not just what they think will go over well.

3. If communication flows freely, decisions will be made with the participation of everyone who has something to offer and the probability that they'll be accepted will increase.

4. Commitment will grow spectacularly for each member of the team when decisions are made.

5. If you achieve commitment, you'll see positive attitudes and a desire to do things. The results will follow.

And then you will have achieved leadership.

14

Articulating

If you want to get out of a hole, first, stop digging.

—Anonymous

What Is Articulating?

Leading a team always means managing change. When we act as a team, we produce results that cause change in the environment, and in so doing, we also change: We learn, experience frustration, grow, and suffer. Outward changes are accompanied by inward changes. The very act of setting a goal for ourselves starts to change us!

In this whole change process, it's fundamentally important to reduce uncertainty to keep everyone's minds open and creative. As a result, their attitudes will be as proactive as possible. This, then, is an essential function of leadership and articulating is a very powerful tool to achieve this.

> Let's refer to articulating as creating a picture of the situation in the minds of the team that will allow them to understand and accept it. This reduces the feeling of uncertainty—the smaller it is, the more trust grows and fear shrinks—and opens their minds to acceptance. Only when we accept something are we able to consider how to change it.

Acceptance is essential to effectively mobilize a team, because our brain's first tendency is to refuse to accept those things that go against our perception. Our initial impulse is to maintain that perception, and we only change it when it's clear that doing so is the only recourse. Best case, this phenomenon slows down and limits the team's ability to respond. Worst case, the team can end up making decisions that are completely removed from the reality of the situation, even though they match the virtual reality that they've created. So the sooner they accept a situation, the sooner they'll be able to manage it and themselves.

As we have seen repeatedly throughout these pages, acceptance is necessary because it is the pavement over which proactivity is built: Only when I accept a situation for what it is can I start to consider how I would like it to be, and then create a plan to make that a reality. Remembering the words of Jung, "what you resist, persists and what you accept, changes."

How It's Done

Shaping a situation requires supplying the team with all the necessary—and properly structured—information in a way that makes everyone feel included and creates an atmosphere of mutual trust. This is very important because in most pressure situations you have to tell people things they do not want to hear, especially when they need to give it their best. If there is any suspicion or mistrust, the dominant mentality will be defensive, which will make creating constructive perspectives even more difficult and, as a result, drag the team away from acceptance.

When you find yourself having to articulate, it will probably be under a double pressure: The one inherent to the situation you face plus the one that comes from assuming the responsibility of motivating the team. Both will cause your insecurities and fears to flare up. In these situations, one of the main fears will be fear of giving information, either because you think of it as "sensitive information that others shouldn't have," or because you want to protect the team from "things that could affect their morale." We are all aware of the dangers that come with giving out certain information, but are we aware of the risks of keeping things from people? How many times have we made things worse by not communicating sufficiently? Make no mistake, when you leave things out your people will fill in the blanks for themselves and I guarantee that what they come up with will be much worse than what you would have told them! In these circumstances, people apply the saying "think the worst and you won't be disappointed." You know that the human brain is a prediction machine. It spends its time generating expectations about what could happen, and always with a negative bias.

A negative thought in our brains weighs more than a positive one.

If one of our ancestors walked through the woods and didn't notice a magnificent piece of fruit, they would lose an opportunity. But if they didn't see the snake nearby, they'd be dead! As Gil Grissom, a character on the TV show *CSI: Las Vegas*, put it, "if, while walking through the savannah, you noticed a breeze at your back, it could be the wind or a predator. We're descendants of those who turned back to check." Fear is in our genes and it has played a fundamental role in the proliferation of our species. You have probably reached adulthood and are reading these pages today because this mechanism has yielded good results in some dangerous situations throughout your life.

It is so easy for us to be aware of certain risks and yet we are so unaware of the dangers of not managing them well. It is so easy to imagine the dangers of giving out information and so hard to realize the dangers of keeping that information from others. This is another leadership challenge: managing your own emotions in order to say what needs to be said, and not just what will go over well. When you communicate, if you do it honestly and confidently, your team will feel like you count on them, and that in and of itself will inspire. It will make them feel capable and elevate them above being just passive victims of the circumstances.

On the contrary, if they feel—correctly or not—that they're being kept in the dark, the team will fall into a vicious circle of self-destruction: They'll lose faith in you and themselves, their commitment will dwindle, fear and defensive behavior (toxic behavior, cliques, and similar) will increase, and this will breed mistrust. The situation could spiral downward quickly. Experienced managers know how quickly this phenomenon can manifest itself. It's stunning! So in order to avoid it, you must articulate as best you can, decisively and confidently. Logically, we have made the leader the focal point of this section. But bear in mind that articulating should also include useful information that comes from the team. It's very important to remember that the leader's role is not just to communicate things to others but also, and most importantly, to ensure that information flows freely between members of the team.

Also, articulating effectively means creating tangible structures: Without boring people with details, use diagrams, summaries, and mental maps and do it on a whiteboard when possible. Use computers sparingly. Limit PowerPoint presentations. Use them only to explain certain complex points; leadership moves on an emotional level, so keep away from reading dozens of slides! Above all, speak and listen! And then, listen some more. Convene your team and face the blank page together. Work on the whiteboard and the flipchart together. Create your own diagrams. Ask a lot of questions, then listen some more, and pay attention to what they tell you. Include people on your team in designing plans and making decisions.

When you think that you alone should be the one making a decision, take the time to explain to your team which parts of it will apply to them and why. And establish a final structure, a diagram or table that sums up your plan of action. Then ask for the team to collaborate and work together to figure out how to put that into practice. Do not be swayed by the pressure of the situation. We know that leadership is not easy.

If you don't know how to do this, get some training or hire a coach. Everything you can do to improve in this area is an excellent investment that will save you an enormous amount of time and energy in the immediate future, during implementation, when real problems arise, and when you need the commitment of others. Most importantly, if you articulate well, you will have taken a giant step toward gaining your team's commitment. This will feed their proactivity, which leads to innovation and creative solutions. Without these, results in an atmosphere of change are impossible.

Articulating a Negative Vision to Facilitate Acceptance

In your time as a manager, you will find that the most frequent situations are the ones in which people are very far from accepting the need or importance of what you are trying to tell them. They probably have no desire to do what you're asking and you may feel like a real spoilsport. In these situations, you will find it very useful to create a negative vision of the future. You can use everything we discussed in the chapter on vision, with one notable difference: You will create a vision of the worst future imaginable, one that is inevitable if they continue with their way of doing things. It should be a negative vision capable of stirring a therapeutic fear—as Italian psychologist Giorgio Nardone would put it—that opens their eyes to the danger they refuse to see. This vision will be very useful in changing the team's individual perspectives, but two conditions are critical:

- It should be logical and plausible based on the situation that the team is seeing. If it doesn't seem like a coherent and probable evolution of the situation, they will be skeptical and you could be seen as a manipulator, a false prophet of the apocalypse. This can damage your credibility and, ultimately, your leadership.

- In your nonverbal communication, you should demonstrate absolute conviction that what you are describing will happen if nothing is done to avoid it. You will have to put it all—all of your *authority*—on the line!

Always remember that this negative vision only serves to uncover the team's perception of things and that way disable the behaviors that it provokes, but this alone will not motivate people. For that you will have to follow up with a positive and constructive vision that inspires hope and energizes people.

15

Normalizing

What Is Normalizing?

Normalizing refers to a key leadership action and one that rarely gets the recognition it deserves. It is a direct descendant of the action of articulating and its goal is also to facilitate the process of acceptance among the team. Articulation should be accompanied by normalization. The former defines the situation and the latter is what allows it to evolve from a feeling of uncertainty, confusion, or blockage to a new normalcy—"is it normal for this to affect me this way?" This is necessary to go from "why is this happening to us?" to "what can we do about it?" Normalizing helps to take us from being victims to heroes.

Because we can only manage what we're aware of, and what we're unaware of manages us, confronting any situation requires that you first become aware of it. The process moves from articulating it to, ultimately, normalizing it. In summary, the sequence goes like this:

1. **Articulating:** This is the situation I am living, this is really happening. I need to look at things as openly and completely as possible, including the things I would rather not see! This is exactly what we described in the previous chapter.

Fear and insecurity, and their offspring, reinforcement and pride, make us see a deformed version of the world. In trying to protect our fragile self-esteem, they sentence us to a deformed perception. Indeed, one of the greatest competitive advantages for highly effective teams is the superior ability of members to help one another avoid these limiting visions.

2. **Normalizing:** How I see this situation. Here we take another step from looking outward—what events are taking place—to looking inward at ourselves: "How is what's happening affecting me?" "How do I feel?" We are moving toward what is essentially an emotional level.

   It's not possible to accept a situation without first accepting our own emotions. That is the essence of normalizing: accepting that it is normal for certain events to produce fear, anxiety, and distress. It's a very important step because awareness of how we react to certain events is the launch pad for deciding how we want to live them. Whenever I am unable to decide how to experience a situation, that situation ends up deciding for me!

Normalize to Achieve Acceptance

Our upbringing has conditioned us to control our emotions—and control always comes with repression—rather than managing them, listening to, accepting, and using them for our own benefit. Since the dawn of time, human beings have been trained—and developed biological automation—to respond quickly to fear stimuli, but not to question alternative ways to respond to them.

Good normalization lets us substantially modify our automatic response patterns. When our emotions shout out at us, rather than ignoring them—falsely believing that if we don't listen to them, they don't exist—we should listen to them and give them their due. We must pay attention to our fears and insecurities because they have a message for us: They tell us what we want to protect ourselves from.

Fear doesn't kill; what kills is fear of fear.

Fear of fear is what makes us reject it. And he who is not afraid is not brave, but unconscious. Being afraid is normal. It's in our genetic programming. In order for our team to grow they must consciously accept fear and insecurity, listen to them carefully, and convert them into a reason to learn. Together with our team, let's consider those emotions and shine a conscious light on them. When we have properly aired them out, we will have a reaction—a turning point—that will make us say, "I've had enough! So now what?"

In my professional experience, I have found that this reaction—when you consciously confront fear—always shows up. Generally, it comes from one of the more combative members of the team—and that will, for a moment, make that person the leader of the reaction. You must, once again, trust the team. And if it doesn't happen spontaneously, it should be the leader's mission to provoke it. Connection with the team is the foundation of leadership and a good leader feels when the moment's right. Don't be afraid to create a situation, to call a meeting, where people can open up! In the articulating process that we've described, you'll find various opportunities. Take advantage of them.

From the team's emotional turning point on, responsiveness will multiply: We will have achieved emotional acceptance and that will provide a clear view of the situation and an open, creative attitude. We will have turned a limit, a roadblock, into a learning opportunity. This is incredibly powerful: what felt like an end becomes the starting point of a new game!

When the team doesn't normalize, it settles into resistance and sets in motion the three known avoidance behaviors, the automatic responses that we have developed as reactions to any threat:

- **I resist,** which often causes even more pressure—"Don't want one? Here's two."

- **I evade,** or I disconnect, as the saying goes, which distances me from the situation and damages my ability to manage.

- **I freeze up,** which limits my ability to understand what's happening and hinders me from focusing on finding creative solutions.

In contrast, acceptance of emotions opens up a different possibility: We can stay focused and calm with a clear mind that lets us identify opportunities and find creative solutions. Where there is creativity, there is growth. John Grinder, one of the pioneers of neuro-linguistic programming, said, "If I have one option, I'm a robot. If I have two, I have a dilemma. If I have three, I am free."

Note! The importance of normalization is that if we achieve acceptance on an intellectual level, but not an emotional one, we end up with resignation rather than true acceptance. On the surface, it may seem like acceptance, but it's radically different: We're really still in the "I don't want it" phase, in pain. We feel like victims of the circumstances, and that leads us to tolerance, which is what resignation is really good for. However, what we need today when faced with uncertainty is to stop being passive victims and start being proactive because our ability to act will change completely. Basically, if our brain understands that we must accept things but our heart doesn't want to, we will experience a state of dissonance that will inevitably lead to a lack of mental clarity and energy. Our behavior will be confused and half-hearted and, in the short-term, we'll suffer from stress. In contrast, when we truly accept a situation, our brain and heart want the same thing—they're properly aligned—and we experience a state of resonance: We will be able to consider the alternatives and imagine how to turn those into realities. We will be proactive!

Is this not what Viktor Frankl advocated in his impressive work *Man's Search for Meaning* (1984) when, analyzing his harrowing experience in a

Nazi concentration camp during World War II, he affirms that "the last of human freedoms is to choose one's attitude"?

Nothing, except maybe our own ignorance and habit, can steal from us the freedom to decide how we want to live a certain situation. The beauty of it is that it's a skill you can learn! There are various techniques to acquire it—many of which are based on neuro-linguistic programming—but demonstrating them is outside the scope of this book.

Acceptance sets our brain to the on-position to confront change! If a leader wants to mobilize his team in a time of crisis, he should get them to accept the crisis and then the entire range of their fears, pains, and insecurities that will inevitably follow. To do this, he'll need to normalize. From that moment on—and not a moment sooner—he can focus the group's energy toward finding ways to move forward: Now you've got them in action!

Pay Attention to the Wrong Questions

When insecurity in search of certainty controls us, thought becomes our enemy.
—Jiddu Krishnamurti

When you lack normalization, situations often arise where the team goes into an infinite loop, to borrow an IT expression. We can understand the need to confront a change on a rational mental level, but the uncertainty we feel can drag us down in search of a false sense of security. Before we can act, we start an endless process of rationally seeking a sense of security that we can't find on an emotional level. It's a dead end, a process known as "paralysis by analysis," that causes us to miss a great deal of opportunities.

In fact, it's the team equivalent of the pathological obsessive doubt that happens in people. It's a problem of intelligence: using reason to resolve problems that don't belong to that sphere. The cause can be found in raising seemingly rational questions that really aren't rational at all, and which have no satisfactory answer. As philosopher Immanuel Kant put it, "it is not possible to respond correctly to an incorrect question." The problem is in the question, not the answer.

Here's a more enlightening example: We're going to launch a new product and we want to be sure that it goes well. If we ask ourselves, "how can we reduce the risk of failure?" (a correct question) the answer could be, for example, conduct a market study (a correct answer). But if we pose the question another way, for example, "how can we have full assurance that it will go well?" we would be facing an incorrect question. Can the market study take all the necessary factors into account? Are we sure that another competitor isn't doing something that could alter the market we plan to conduct the study in? Or wouldn't we lose valuable time and alert the competition of our actions, ultimately making the actual launch conditions obsolete? We would be charging a bottomless battery of questions that, rather than reducing insecurity, would increase it and do nothing but lead to more questions. In fact, the only correct response to that question would be to think that "we can't answer it because we'll never be positive that the launch will be a success," accept that, and risk it.

The leader can only have one reaction to an incorrect question: Bring it before the team and resist answering it. Make people aware that the question comes from insecurity and emotions, and that the answer must be found there. And, as we have seen, this can only mean accepting that insecurity.

> When the team goes into an infinite loop, it's the leader's mission to make them see that they are proposing questions that have no answers so they accept their insecurity and start managing it.

The leader will do this by using authority and leading by example. If the leader is able to absorb uncertainty and stay positive, the message to the team will be "Follow me. It doesn't matter what's actually out there. We'll never know for sure anyway and we can only act on what we think we should be doing." If the leader acts with conviction and is a living example of it, the team will move past doubt and into action. They will focus on what they should do. It works.

16

Developing People

A man should never be appointed to a managerial position if his vision focuses on people's weaknesses rather than on their strengths.
—Peter Drucker, *Drucker Management*

We are all very ignorant. What happens is that not all ignore the same things.
—Albert Einstein

Learn as if you were to live forever. Live as if you were to die tomorrow.
—Charles Chaplin

One of leadership's most powerful tools is knowing how to connect a team's challenges to each individual's professional and personal development. That means turning experiences that they're willing to have into learning opportunities: "If you do this a certain way, you not only contribute to the team's success, but you will learn this or grow professionally in this way."

It relates to what Goleman, Boyatzis, and McKee define in their book *Primal Leadership* (2002) as the leader coach, whose contribution is one of the most effective for team atmosphere and development.

Contrary to popular belief, it's a proven fact that learning in companies is not automatic or intrinsic. Working hard doesn't mean learning. It's not enough because learning requires proactivity: You have to want to learn in order to achieve it. Many organizations lack policies that support it, with notable exceptions—especially in more knowledge-dependent industries—because results are usually the only requirement. People aren't expected to learn from them.

In my time as a consultant, I have frequently come across business veterans who would say things to me like, "I have 15 years of industry experience." But watching them in action I would think, "this guy has one year of experience repeated 15 times." How much time do you dedicate to reviewing your own work, to identifying areas of improvement, to innovation? Where does the proverb "man is the only animal that trips over the same stone twice" come from?

The mere passing of time will make you older, but not wiser.

In order for an experience to equal real knowledge, it requires active analysis, structuring, and consideration of new alternatives. This effort is what illuminates learning and allows us to transform, like modern-day alchemists, the raw lead of experience-living into the gold of experience-knowing or true Experience, with a capital E. This process is rarely intuitive—people are often unaware of it—meaning that managers must make sustained efforts to create awareness and incorporate learning into the corporate culture. This includes developing habits and mechanisms that force teams out of the trenches to look at the battlefield and their own behavior from above, and in doing so consider new paths for growth.

Of course, it's difficult and uncertain for this to yield short-term gains. We find ourselves in a classic conflict: Prioritize between what's urgent and what's important. It's tempting to postpone any effort that, despite its significance to the company's future, doesn't help to immediately put the company in the black. One variable that aggravates the situation is high management turnover, because who wants to put in all that effort for someone else to reap the rewards?

Another added difficulty is completely psychological: pressure for short-term results, the trimming of management teams and increased workload of the remaining ones, all turns teams into firefighting specialists and creates an addiction to emergency and adrenaline. When we're under its subtle influence, we get the sense that if we're not solving problems, we're not working. As a result, we end up recognizing work as just solving specific problems, and we stop thinking strategically. From here, how can work be a creative and constructive activity? Where are the mission and vision? Answer: on that corporate website that no one ever looks at—even if they do look very nice there—or hung up in a dusty frame near the coffee machine.

It takes high-quality leadership and a lot of perseverance to create a corporate culture that focuses on learning. What's more, you need a permanently watchful eye to preserve it. No backsliding!

So, we've already looked at the difficulties, but we should also mention the rewards. Surely, at some point in our careers we have all experienced that addiction to emergency caused by endless, intense activity that numbs and frees us from thought and which ultimately buries us in the void of routine. Having experienced that feeling opens many people up to valuing things that reinvigorate and give meaning back to their work (and their lives). They will be ready to feel the emotional satisfaction that comes from professional development and to turn their role into a growth opportunity.

The essence of success that developing people offers comes from getting them to learn and enjoy their work, helping them find meaning and satisfaction in it, and substantially increase their commitment.

An Important Point of Clarification

At this point we need to make something clear: The leader coach is not a coach. Some confusion has developed around this topic, in part from coaching institutions in search of students, that is blurring the real role of the leader coach. Let's clear that up. A coach is a professional who accompanies and helps their client know himself better, to create a plan for his life, and carry that plan out. The relationship between a coach and her client is one of equals, colleagues, where the client is the decision maker. The coach doesn't lead her client. The client doesn't follow the coach. It's a shared leadership relationship.

A leader coach, by definition, acts in a leadership capacity and the team follows. It is not a shared leadership relationship. A leader identifies the potential within his team and ties their challenges and tasks to their learning, as well as their personal and professional growth. The leader knows how to inspire them to do things and, ultimately, creates and maintains the context they need to do it.

How to Be a Leader Coach

If you'd like to lead this way, you will have to learn to focus on what your team is and what they could be: Go beyond fixing shortcomings to concentrate on developing people's strengths, as Peter Drucker said in the quote at the beginning of this chapter. It's a demanding job for which you should be fully prepared.

To start with, you should know the members of your team very well. You have to develop trust by spending time with them, being genuinely interested in them, and actively listening to them. You will also need to keep your mind open to new perspectives and get past simple daily tasks to uncover potential talents that they are, surely, not exercising on a daily basis. In a way, you'll have to make the effort to rediscover the people around you. Remember that it's always hardest to look at people in a new light when they are very close to you, but you must develop new perspectives. For that reason, even if it's not an absolute necessity, you will find the services of a coach to be immensely helpful.

As you discover their potential, that treasure trove of talent, you can stimulate their creativity and make it easier for them to find ways to apply their potential to their challenges and tasks. You will then have the basis for approaching the owners of those talents with offers such as "if you do it this way, the team can gain this and you will learn how to do this or you will develop this skill."

17

Harmonizing

The systemic function of leadership is to make members of the team resonate along a longitudinal wavelength to boost them toward a common goal, fostering the growth of synergies and creativity. To harmonize people in a human system you need to focus attention on the relationships between them: First you need to build them or, if they already exist, fortify them.

This part will be more important the more diverse the team is. The more diversity, the more value there is in bringing teammates together. Teams today face a complexity far beyond obvious factors such as age, educational background, or gender. They are more multicultural and are often geographically isolated from one another without the benefit of sharing a common physical space.

Since the dawn of time, human beings have seen, smelled, and touched one another. We have spoken face to face and shared food around the campfire. These primitive mechanisms for creating harmony are how we build trust. They express what we have been for thousands of years. Now we have to create trust with people who are different from us, with little to no time for direct personal interaction, and in an atmosphere of accelerated change. It's not easy to get to know people in this context, when doing so has always meant sharing emotions in close quarters.

Building relationships between members of the team, creating time and space for sincere contact, and maintaining an atmosphere that fosters harmony are valuable skills in a leader today. These things require a strong capacity for empathy and an ability to communicate throughout the organization the importance of investing time and resources, in what professor Peter Cappelli of the Wharton School of Management called relationship capital.

The latter of these is self-explanatory: Despite all the talk within companies about "how important it is to get to know one another," there are many people who think that relational activities are a waste of time. The "we're here to work and not waste time on nonsense" mentality is alive and well in many organizations. This seemingly rationalist mindset is the biggest enemy of trust development in a team because it limits the inclination toward giving importance to relationships and discourages those who wish to do so.

Let's recall that pretending that emotions don't matter doesn't make them disappear, they just go into hiding where they can bring us down from the shadows. We could go on learning to control our emotions, victory after victory until we are finally defeated by stress, an internal void, or even depression. This supposed rationalism is often simply a mask for fear of our emotions!

Fear of Emotions

Fear of emotions causes strange situations. I once helped transform a very enterprising and energetic general manager. He would constantly harass his team with ideas, projects, instructions, and mandates. Exhaustion spread and key executives felt overwhelmed, with little room to grow. Some were already entertaining the possibility of leaving the company.

Through an executive coaching program, working on himself intensely —like all things he did—our subject found that he was really just bored with himself. He was bored of the character that had been built up over time.

Among other things, he decided to be less authoritarian and more of a people supporter. Surprisingly, when he started to work toward those objectives, several members of his team started provoking him. These were the same people who had complained about him being a dictator, and now they wanted him to pick up the whip! They were invoking the person he had been and discouraging the one he wanted to be.

I have witnessed this phenomenon on several occasions: When we make a change, the people closest to us feel an emotional impact that increases their insecurity. They sense that we're acting weird and want us to go back to normal. I call this event "the challenge of the addict who returns to the old neighborhood," because it reminds me of what happens when, after undergoing detox, an addict returns to his environment: His friends offer him free drugs and he must overcome this pitfall to avoid relapse.

The meaning behind this phenomenon is clear: When a personal change starts to become tangible, we subconsciously become a sort of radio beacon that broadcasts two very powerful messages. First, change is possible; we are living proof. Second and a consequence of the first, the people around us are faced with their own challenge—"if change is possible, he is achieving it and I am not even trying"—which causes strong dissonance. To stop this, we see a subconscious, defensive response that seeks to thwart this uncomfortable process—"if he goes back to being who he was, things will be as they were and I'll stop questioning myself." It makes sense. They didn't ask for this change. It was just thrown into their laps. When we make a personal change, we are indirectly inducing a change in others!

In systemic terms, we'll see this resistance phenomenon as a manifestation of the principle of homeostasis, which functions to get the system back to its former state of balance. From this perspective, a personal change—and more so for a key manager—is always a systemic process. If the person leading the change perseveres, she could thrust the system into a new state, which should also create a new state of balance. On the other hand, she will face environmental resistance and won't get much help. Quite the opposite. She will need to find supporters. Thus it is important to involve others, gain their understanding, and get them to help. If she can't, she has to choose to hinder her own change process, make changes to her environment, or change environments all together. In business scenarios, the manager may be faced with the decision to leave the company. She could also feel the need to change some members of the team—possible and painful—but if we're talking about a family situation, this will be nearly impossible. And then there's the scenario that includes both of these cases, like in a family-run business.

How to Harmonize

The reaction we've described is one of the main difficulties to overcome during any process of change. It requires a person's total conviction in the necessity of the change and a trust in his own strengths. But it also requires faith that those around him will be able to accept it. It's a tremendous trial by fire for personal leadership: getting people to understand it, accept it, and help you succeed. The team must also be in harmony with themselves and with the change itself. As we have seen, this is a major challenge. Empathy in this situation will be the key that opens the door to emotions and, as a result, the team will feel the change collectively.

Empathy builds a common emotional base on which the team will communicate. If we want to create harmony between people, we must know how the situation is affecting them. They should talk sincerely, share, agree, and commit. It's not enough to simply create moments and activities to help align people. They need to be imbued with genuine emotional content. Without empathy, the team faces the question, "we're already together, now what?" How many meals and company events have turned into tedious obligations, empty carcasses infested with "cocktail smiles!"

Knowing how to foster emotional discovery and exchange is one of the distinctive traits that Goleman, Boyatzis, and McKee (2002) have called affiliative leadership style, the vocation of which we described at the start of this chapter. To get it to effectively contribute to the team's performance, it should be based on the leader's capacity for empathy—founded in a sincere interest in people—and his clear commitment to the team by being the first to put himself out there and take the first step.

18

Facing Conflict

When we talk about teams in conflict, we really mean teams that don't face conflicts, but rather avoid and postpone them until things ultimately boil over. Then we see selfishness and toxic behaviors inundate the team. The group atmosphere suffers and the future becomes very bleak.

However, experience shows that even if it seems counterintuitive, the teams that work well are those that face their conflicts. They act on a solid foundation of trust that helps them put egos aside for the good of the group and, in that way, address conflict from a constructive perspective. Everyone feels like they are a part of the process and people aren't afraid to speak up. As a result, information is shared, ideas flow freely, no one feels attacked, and decision making is healthy. This causes people to identify with certain decisions, which is that long sought-after state of commitment!

When that foundation of trust isn't there, people don't play fair with information—thinking "information is power" or "I'll share what I need to"—and, as a consequence, commitment to the team and its decisions dwindles. Everyone puts their own interests above those of the group. I feel bad for those kinds of teams. And, similarly, one might feel bad for those societies that are unable to build or nurture this vision of community.

Ego is our individual survival software: Its job is to make us feel unique and feel like we can overcome others to survive. It's a powerful tool that, in theory, works to our benefit so that we can survive successfully. But we still don't quite know how to control it very well and it often overpowers us. That's when we end up working for our own ego: to be the wealthiest, most attractive, most popular, the one with the fastest car, or the most attractive couple.

Our ego is necessary and important, but we are not our ego. We are more than that. That's why ego management is a key element of leadership: To lead, you need a powerful ego, but you also have to keep it in check; make it work for you rather than against you. In short, the conflict paradox means that what are considered teams in conflict are the ones that in reality avoid conflict. When that foundation of trust is missing, suspicion and insecurity increase, people hide who they are and don't let others on the team get to know them. The behavior of others is seen through a defensive lens and is automatically assumed to be negative—remember, "think the worst and you won't be disappointed."

We know that "things can go sour fast," and, deep down, "we're just here to work," we don't want to "make waves" and we remember that it's "better the devil you know." And if we think that something could bother someone, but "that causes problems," we end up keeping our mouths shut—"we don't get paid for this"—because "that's what the boss is for." Basically, we fear engaging in delicate subjects; we sweep disagreements under the rug as if they never happened, even though they clearly do; we don't question how we work; and all of this means that there is no learning at all. We create a perverse dynamic of concealment, alienation, and toxicity where conflicts are avoided until the atmosphere is suffocating and conflict inevitably breaks out. Ah! At that point, we can clearly see a team in conflict. However, that wasn't the moment the conflict started. It was just the moment it was harvested after being planted a long time ago.

> Managers are rarely aware of the fact that, when we don't fight conflict avoidance clearly and decidedly, we're really sanctioning a terrible process that deforms and miseducates our teams.

Then what should we do? Being aware of this phenomenon, making it clear to the team, and facilitating constructive conflict management are fundamental tasks for a leader. This requires a lot of mettle and vigilance because of how easily we fall into self-deception. But above all, because initially, a conflict often seems insignificant, there are always more pressing priorities, and it's very tempting to defer addressing it. For example: "it's not that big a deal," "there are more important priorities right now," "they're all adults, they can handle it," and "I don't have time for this" are all common excuses.

The challenge that these situations pose for a leader is that they are often unrewarding. They force you to wade through the muck, challenge beliefs—"personal relationships are always a complicated waste of time"—and, in fact, no conflict has really even happened yet. At least this is how we want to see it because we can't clearly see the long-term consequences.

The Treatment

Getting the team to address their conflicts demands a lot of authority and courage on your part. That's because it requires you to take a whole series of sustained and harmonized actions, on yourself and others:

- **Manage your own ego.** If we're talking from our ego, we give the impression that we're "out for ourselves." In contrast, if we can talk sincerely from a perspective of the good of the team, we bolster our leadership.

- **Encourage cohesion** between teammates so that trust can grow between them. Feel free to organize situations, at work and outside work, so that the team can get to know each other, share experiences, and, basically, to take care of itself.

- **Develop a cooperative culture in the team,** going against the traditional paradigm of fostering competition between teammates. And run from the Machiavellian "divide and conquer" like a bat out of hell: Today, success and hard work belong to everyone, so it's important to achieve synergy through cooperation.

- **Work on basic values that promote trust** such as respect, generosity, and humility. As a leader, you should be a living example of these values.

- **Create an open learning culture.** People should learn to take risks and fail well to experience true learning. Relish the opportunity to congratulate those who take risks and go off the beaten path. Establish incentives for those who learn from their mistakes, even if they didn't get the results they were looking for—or maybe because they didn't!

- **Fight fear of rejection and failure.** Engage in constructive criticism publicly, decisively, clearly, and forcefully with anyone who uses the mistakes of others to deride them.

- **Train your team on how to ask for help, offer help, and flag problems.** These things seem very basic but, believe me, we tend to do them very poorly. You couldn't imagine the number of problems they cause. Of course, we aren't born with the knowledge of how to do them effectively.

- **Work on how to give and receive feedback** and train your team in these skills. Everything from the previous item applies here. Our feedback is generally pretty poor. It mixes emotions and judgments and is so full of personal critiques that the recipient is forced to defend himself rather than focus on improvement.

- **Promote open and constructive dialogue about seemingly negative experiences.** As Peter Senge (1990) wrote: "For the Greeks, dialogue meant the free flow of meaning throughout the group, which allows the group to discover perspectives that aren't possible for the individual. . . . Dialogue differs from 'discussion,' which literally means 'batting' ideas around in a winner-take-all competition. The discipline in dialogue also means recognizing patterns of interaction that erode learning within the team. These defense patterns are often deeply rooted in how the team works. If left unidentified, they undermine learning. If you do identify them and let them grow creatively, they can actually accelerate learning."

Preparing your team to deal with conflicts constructively will be one of the most intense exercises a leader can engage in, one that will also contribute the most to your leadership development. You will also very quickly notice the effect it has on the team's efficiency and overall team atmosphere. It is, without a doubt, a genuine touchstone that distinguishes great leaders and puts them on a higher leadership pedestal.

Conclusion

Is It Better to Lead
Than Command?

Over the course of these pages, we have seen how leadership is practiced from the self, from who we are. If you live it from a place of awareness, it can become a path of personal growth, both when it is practiced and when it is lost. Leadership is a difficult and rare skill. Organizations should consider it an endangered species, supporting its growth and prohibiting its extinction. This species' natural habitat is very subtle: It's that delicate, razor-thin line that exists between self-leadership and the impact it has on others. To inhabit that space for a while is like getting a master's in human nature.

We now also know that leadership is not a quality that only certain individuals possess. Instead, it is relational by nature. And creating a context in which constructive relationships can start and develop is an essential part of the art of managing people.

We have seen how this requires managers to successfully manage their egos, both to lead and to allow others to lead. They must also have the conscience and courage to revise certain paradigms and beliefs that until now have seemed immovable, which we have referred to here as ideas that do not help.

The ultimate goal of leadership is to get the team to give the best of themselves in the pursuit of a predefined goal in spite of uncertainty. We're talking about a systemic role that not only contributes to the result, but also dignifies the group because it nurtures key values like generosity and humility. In short, good leadership goes beyond success to make us better, help us grow, give our work meaning, and enrich our perception.

Every day we see how business sectors where the routine once prevailed and people could employ authoritarian management styles are undergoing violent, disruptive changes that make leadership styles that can open people's minds necessary. Of course, the use of formal power is still needed, but it is less and less adequate to meet these challenges.

Our organizations are traveling at the speed of light from an old planet in which people do things, toward a new world that considers getting people to "want to do" a critical factor. It is a place where people are expected to put their bodies, hearts, and minds into their work.

As uncertainty grows, attitudes such as flexibility, creativity, and relationship management are more important than ever to finding your way out of the darkness and living a happier, low-stress life.

Today we inhabit a world of accelerated technological change that creates a context where our 1,000-year-old survival mechanisms are actually counterproductive, perhaps for the first time in recorded history. We need new resources that empower us to successfully unravel uncertainty and complexity. And we aren't born with these resources. We have to learn them. We now know how leadership helps us to develop them. We know that the answer to greater uncertainty is, without a doubt, more and better leadership!

So, is it better to lead than command?

The answer is clear: It is better to lead than command!

Acknowledgments

When I began writing these pages, I experienced firsthand how a more or less creative act, regardless of its quality, can completely "abduct you" and isolate you from your surroundings. Therefore, my first acknowledgment goes, without a doubt, to Maribel, my wife and companion in everything—including, of course, this work—and to my daughter, Raquel, who have most directly suffered the consequences of this project and the obsessions that came with it.

I am also grateful to my editor, Virtuts Angulo, and her team at Libros de Cabecera, for their faith in this book and their professional excellence. Virtuts knows how to inspire, energize, give confidence, and pose questions. She also knows when to accept the things that seem important to an author and are sometimes hard to understand. She is a true partner!

My complete gratitude to professor Ricard Serlavós for his faith in this work's potential, which reinforced my own at a key moment in my life. And, of course, I am especially thankful for his graciousness in writing such an inspiring foreword, which helps the reader gain a clear perspective of what leadership means.

A very special thanks also to Richard Boyatzis, Jesús Serafín Pérez, Santi Freixa, and David Caminada, who were kind enough to read the manuscript and offer their opinions on it.

Having said all that, I would like to thank:

- The good leaders I have had the pleasure of knowing, some firsthand and others at a distance, for everything they have taught me that brought me into this intangible arena. Thanks to you all! I wish there were more of you! The world could use more leadership!

- To all the bad bosses and mediocre leaders I have suffered through over the years. I've learned a lot from you about the influence that bad decisions and bad attitudes have on people. Still, you were the first victims of those actions, given that behind the abuse of power lies insecurity and fear. I wish that this book could help you in some way.

- To a particularly bad boss who "got me off the street" and, without meaning to, put me on a path that opened my eyes. Thanks. I now know that back then I had the raw material necessary to become someone like him.

- To my students for having faith in me, for not having faith in me, for believing me, for not believing me, and for testing me. And, above all, for making me feel like I could really help others. I am especially grateful to everyone who had the courage and generosity to express their doubts and their vulnerability. Thank you for that authentic leadership that helped us all learn from it.

- To my dear Barcelona, beautiful and inspiring, open to the world, great stomach that digests it all, source of innovation and enterprise. Poor, lonely Barcelona!

Last but not least, I am very thankful for the good and bad leader that I have turned out to be, sometimes all at once! When I began leading teams, people barely got any leadership training. You just did it. That gives me the dubious honor of knowing that there isn't a single subject in this book that I haven't fumbled through at least once in my career—often more than once. I've capitalized from all this background, which I later reflected on, learned from, and passed on, but I had such a hard time in those early moments!

Appendix:
Exercises to Start
Connecting With the Self

The longest journey is the one that leads back to your doorstep.

—Chinese proverb

Throughout this work, we have seen how leadership is practiced from the self. That's why we have seen many situations that require us to be present and connected with ourselves in each situation that we are managing in order to get the impact we seek.

In life, we often discover that the biggest advancements come from small steps. The purpose of this appendix is to put those small steps within reach of the reader so that they may carry you very far. We will lay out a series of simple exercises that can help you achieve a mental and emotional state that supports that connection and, thus, achieve positive results. These are exercises that the reader can do on their own without a coach or trainer.

They can be used to overcome specific situations, as they arise or at a predetermined time, but doing them effectively requires continual practice. If we get in the habit of doing certain small things that raise our awareness and help us stay present on a daily basis, we can greatly increase our effectiveness. There is a very clear metaphor that applies to this: If a great golfer and a mediocre golfer both swing their drivers at the same time, their balls will probably land hundreds of yards apart, but at the moment that each one took a swing, the difference in the angle of their drivers was only a few degrees. Small changes in key areas can drastically modify our trajectory.

So we must remember that the purpose of this appendix is both ambitious and deliberately limited: To pique the reader's interest, open the door to this fascinating and increasingly more necessary world of personal management, and let them start on their own path of discovery.

Exercise 1: Connection Through Breathing

When you find yourself under pressure, your mind begins to frantically move from conjuring potential outcomes (prediction) to searching for past resources (remembering) that could be useful now. This results in stress and a loss of intellectual performance. If you can disrupt this process, you will free up your mind and begin to transmit "presentness" and a feeling of being connected. To achieve this, you will have to give yourself a few minutes of isolation. Try it. It's well worth the investment.

1. Sit upright and keep your back loose. Close your eyes. Uncross your arms and legs.

2. Focus your attention on how your body feels. Feel your feet on the ground, your back against the chair, your arms as heavy as lead, and your head up and loose.

3. Concentrate on your breathing. Focus on the area of your body that you can feel most readily: your stomach or your chest.

4. Inhale and exhale naturally. Your goal is not to control, but to contemplate.

When distracting thoughts emerge, accept them as something natural. Contemplate them and let them run their course. They are a normal function of the human mind. Refocus your mind, gently and firmly, on your breathing. Repeat this as needed without obsessing over doing it perfectly: The real learning goal for you will be less about how long you can focus on your breathing and more about knowing how to regain your focus after a distraction. Give yourself 15 to 30 minutes for this exercise. To help you keep your mind off of the time, set up a timer on your watch or phone.

Exercise 2: Conscious Walking

Another way to achieve connection and presence with the self is something as simple as learning to walk consciously. What we do in our daily lives is not really walking, but rather going: Our minds are set on what we have to do, not on what we are doing as we walk. However, walking can be an excellent exercise for connecting with pressure-filled or stressful situations. All you have to do is follow these instructions:

1. Allow at least 15 minutes for this exercise. Isolate yourself and, if possible, go barefoot.

2. Start walking step by step, trying to go as slowly as possible. Focus your attention on every inch of the sole of your foot as it hits the floor.

3. You will probably find it difficult to walk slowly and you will feel off-balance. This is completely normal: The more stressed you are, the more difficult this exercise will be.

4. Don't feel guilty. Keep at it calmly and you will feel your body harmonize itself as the tension dissipates.

I have used this exercise a lot with executives who are under large amounts of pressure and they have seen enormous results. They have noted an increase in their physical awareness and improved connection with themselves. You can use it to focus on targeted situations or just as a daily activity to heighten self-awareness and reduce stress.

Exercise 3: Recharging By Connecting With Personal Values

Values are mental states that give us energy. When what we do, or how we do it, honors a value that we find relevant, we feel a kind of vibration that increases our energy. In contrast, when something tramples a personal value, our energy decreases and we sometimes even feel hurt or angry.

1. We can raise our emotional disposition by connecting with our values, assuming we know how. The main difficulty is that we are largely unaware of our values. We cannot access them through our rational mind: If I ask myself what my values are, the answer will be something of a rational nature that I think sounds appropriate. So, let's try a visualization: Close your eyes and connect with your inner feelings, following the same pattern explained in Exercise 1 for three or four minutes, or until you are ready. You don't have to achieve absolute relaxation, just enough to feel ready to start; you'll know when you're there.

2. In your mind, travel to some moment in your life where everything seemed perfect and you felt completely satisfied. Your age at that time and the activity you were engaged in are irrelevant. Give yourself permission to access your mind naturally without forcing it. It's also unimportant if you find an imaginary situation rather than something you actually experienced. It can even be a mix of situations or situations that aren't exactly like what may have really happened. The only thing that matters is that it evokes that feeling of complete satisfaction.

3. Disconnect your rational mind: Do not analyze or judge, just be with your thoughts. Accept the images and the physical or emotional sensations that may come. Give yourself permission to immerse yourself in all the details of that situation.

4. Focus on the details: Who are you with, what are you doing, what is the environment like, are there any distinct smells? Are there any animals? Any vegetation? Are you in an urban setting?

5. Spend some time in your visualization until you have the feeling that you have discovered everything it has to offer.

6. Make a mental copy of the physical sensation that this visualization has given you.

7. Take a deep breath and open your eyes.

8. Quickly and without thinking, rationally write down everything that seems relevant. Don't worry about order, writing style, or grammar. Your goal is to record the experience with as much detail as possible.

If you do this exercise several times, you may come up with different situations or ones that differ in some way. Don't worry. Just go with it.

A situation that gives us a feeling of complete satisfaction, be it real or imaginary, is full of personal values. What moves us is not the value itself, but rather how we experience it. By invoking that situation, we connect ourselves with our values and our energy levels increase.

The simple act of evoking that situation will be a useful tool for modifying your emotional tone when you need to. It will also come in handy as a happy place in certain situations: For example, if you are waiting to go into an important meeting, rather than letting anxiety overcome you, you can spend that time by connecting with your values, which will let you go into the meeting refreshed with more favorable non-verbal communication.

Exercise 4: Deactivating Fears and Insecurities

We all have thoughts that stop us in our tracks—thoughts that make us feel less capable. These are part of our defensive software, which is designed to protect us from what we subconsciously perceive to be dangerous, even if there is no danger. When we try to control them, they go into hiding, but keep working in the background. We'll call them saboteurs because they are actively sabotaging our plans. Among them, fears and insecurities are the easiest to pinpoint.

These thoughts can be managed with the right techniques. But to do that, you first have to give them a conscious form. Let's give a name and a face to each of them so that we can create a mental entity to have a dialogue with. We want this saboteur to help rather than hurt us. When a saboteur goes unheard, it feels the need to shout louder until our mind becomes so chaotic that we can't make appropriate decisions. But we are going to help it do its job. Then, we'll put it aside long enough for us to make decisions or take actions. Bear in mind that we don't want to get rid of it. We just don't want it to interfere at critical times.

This exercise is more impactful if you capitalize on real thoughts that bring you down, such as fears or insecurities, but you can also conjure them up willingly. Just remember recent situations that caused a relevant emotional impact, as described in the following guide.

1. Think of a situation that provokes a sense of fear, insecurity, or thoughts of discouragement.

2. Disconnect your rational mind: Do not analyze or judge, just be with your thoughts. Accept the images and the physical or emotional sensations that may come. Give yourself permission to immerse yourself in all the details of that situation.

3. Focus your attention on how your body feels. Where on your body is it most noticeable? What is it like? Would you describe it as tension, stinging, or pain? Is it isolated to one area or moving to different locations?

4. Let your mind ascribe a visual metaphor to it, starting with "it's as if . . ." For example, "it's as if a fist were squeezing my heart" or "it's as if a dark fog were surrounding me."

5. Now that you have an image for it, let your mind give this entity a name. Don't force it or distract yourself with finding a logical name. Simply accept what comes to your mind, even if it doesn't make sense. It's fine if you draw a blank. Just keep going anyway.

6. With an open mind and refraining from judgment, address that entity and ask it: "What do you want from me?" and "What do you want for me?" Listen, consider, and accept its response. This could also cause the entity to take on a different form. Understand and accept that it works for you and its mission is to protect you from something it considers dangerous.

7. Express your gratitude.

8. Repeat the process until you feel like you have gotten all the information it had to offer. Don't worry if you don't understand the messages. They will make sense over time.

9. Thank the entity again and send it away somewhere it will find pleasant. Reward it, give it a vacation. It has succeeded in its mission!

Take a deep breath, open your eyes, and take notes to record the experience.

This guide will help us learn to listen to and harmonize our rational mind and our emotions, so that we can be more resonant. Remember that if you analyze or judge what comes to mind, your emotions will go into hiding and you will interrupt the flow of information. Our emotional messages are not logical, but symbolic, and analyzing them won't give us much information in the end.

Exercise 5: Creating an Action Plan From Resonance

This exercise will let us create an action plan from a place of resonance where our emotions are working for us. Let's start with—what else!—a visualization.

As is our custom, we will not judge or analyze, just accept what comes to our imagination. Let's get to it:

1. Take a few deep breaths. Let your body go at its own breathing pace and disconnect your rational thinking for a while.

2. Using your imagination, travel three years forward in time, for example. Imagine as vividly as you can what your ideal life is like. You have achieved everything you dreamed of and your life is satisfying and full of success. Imagine and enjoy this and focus a lot on the details.

3. In your mind, you have achieved everything you wanted! Think about what you are doing, your career, and who you are with. What is the environment like? The scenery? Are there any distinct smells? Music?

4. Now turn your attention to how you feel physically: What is that like? Do you feel light? Serene?

5. Do any images or metaphors come to mind? Living this mental experience intensely is important to what we will do shortly!

6. Take a deep breath, open your eyes, and take some notes to fix your mind in the experience.

Now, from that future of success that you have just visualized, work backward and, quickly and without thinking, write down the answers to the following questions in the order that they appear.

- What am I like and what do I do in my vision?
- What have I had to learn or add to my life (knowledge, attitudes, or habits)?
- What have I had to let go of (ideas, habits, or attitudes)?
- What energizes me?

Write liberally without worrying about grammar or spelling, and try not to worry about whether or not it makes sense. Just write! Surprise yourself with the ideas that come out! Don't lose your connection to the visualization.

Go over the results of this first round. What feelings does it bring up? Have there been any surprises or things that have changed priorities?

Later, you can repeat this a few times more calmly. To distinguish from the results of your first draft, use a different color pen or pencil.

You can use this exercise to create an action plan for your life in general, like the example that we just used. You can also use it for a specific aspect of your life. It's useful in both cases, as long as you manage to create a vivid visualization that is full of emotion. Forget about "what you deserve," "the way things are," and "what's advisable." It's important to set a timeline for yourself that is far enough in the future that you can do the things you want to do, but not so far that you can think, "ah, I'll start next year."

Selected Bibliography

Burleigh, M. 2010. *Moral Combat: Good and Evil in World War II*. London: Harper Press.

Camilly, J., and J. Normand. 1983. *El Arma de vida: el zen y el arte tradicional del Samurai [Weapon of Life: Zen and the Traditional Art of the Samurai]*. Barcelona: Vision Libros.

Damasio, A. 1994. *Descartes' Error: Emotion, Reason, and the Human Brain*. New York: G.P. Putnam's Sons.

Day, D., and R. Lord. 1988. "Executive Leadership and Organizational Performance: Suggestions for a New Theory and Methodology." *Journal of Management* 14(3): 453-464.

Frankl, V.E. 1984. *Man's Search for Meaning*. New York: Simon & Schuster.

Goleman, D., R. Boyatzis, and A. McKee. 2002. *Primal Leadership: Realizing the Power of Emotional Intelligence*. Boston: Harvard Business School Press.

———. 2003. *The New Leaders: Transforming the Art of Leadership*. London: Little Brown.

Jackson, P., and H. Delehanty. 1995. *Sacred Hoops: Spiritual Lessons of a Hardwood Warrior*. New York: Hyperion.

Lencioni, P. 2002. *The Five Dysfunctions of a Team: A Leadership Fabel*. San Francisco: Jossey-Bass.

Maslow, A. 1965. *Eupsychian Management: A Journal*. Homewood, IL: Richard Invin and Dorsey Press.

Michaels, E., H. Handfield-Jones, and B. Axelrod. 2001. *The War for Talent*. Boston: Harvard Business Press.

Rosenthal, R. 1968. *Pygmalion in the Classroom*. New York: Holt, Rinehart and Winston.

Senge, P. 1990. *The Fifth Discipline: The Art and Practice of the Learning Organization*. New York: Doubleday.

Service, R. 2004. *Stalin: A Biography*. London: Macmillan.

Watt, S. 2012. "Deborah Ancona: 'The Myth of the Omniscient and Omnipotent, Leader Ultimately Erodes the Confidence of the People.'" *Harvard Deusto*, January. www.harvard-deusto.com/articulo/Deborah-Ancona-El-mito-del-lider-omnisciente-y-omnipotente-en-ultimo-termino-erosiona-la-confianza-de-las-personas.

About the Author

Jorge Cuervo (Born 1959), has a degree in pharmaceutical sciences and an MBA from ESADE; he is also certified in strategic planning, has a CPCC coaching certificate from CTI, a PCC coaching certification from ICF, graduated in ORSC Coaching for Relational Systems from CRR, and is certified by the Leadership Circle Profile.

For nearly 20 years, he has held marketing and sales management positions in multinational companies. Since 2001, he has been a consultant and trainer specializing in team organization, leadership, and change management. He has been an executive coach and team coach since 2007, working with national and international companies.

He is also a professor of leadership and change management at Barcelona Activa. He contributes to training and postgraduate programs at various universities and chambers of commerce. He has developed unique approaches that combine training and coaching techniques to offer his students resources that more effectively apply on a personal level.

His website is www.versorconsulting.com.